T0127712

Thoughts
for
Meditation

How to Unleash the Power of the Subconscious
Mind to Achieve Success in Any Endeavor

Ari

authorHOUSE®

AuthorHouse™
1663 Liberty Drive
Bloomington, IN 47403
www.authorhouse.com
Phone: 1 (800) 839-8640

Published by AuthorHouse 02/26/2018

ISBN: 978-1-5462-3099-1 (sc)
ISBN: 978-1-5462-3097-7 (hc)
ISBN: 978-1-5462-3098-4 (e)

Library of Congress Control Number: 2018902479

Print information available on the last page.

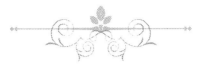

Silence is golden… find a safe quiet place where you can be alone. Make yourself comfortable and let your mind go blank. Focus on your breathing, inhale thru your nose for a four to six count. Then exhale thru your mouth for the same duration. Practice your breathing for about five minutes. It is best to do your meditation in a sitting position, with your feet flat on the floor. Keep your spine straight.

You can clasp your hands (as though in prayer). Or you can rest your hands on your thighs, palms up in supplication. You can meditate in any position. You can tell thru trial and error which position works best for you.

After you have done your breathing, you are ready to do your mantra. Some people use a dead, unintelligible language. For example, they will tell you a certain phrase will give you a sense of inner peace. But why use it when you can do affirmations In English? Simply say: I am at peace with myself, God and the universe; we are one. Other possibilities include: I am one with God. and the universe. There is only one there is only now. Or, God is the light, the light is love. You can think of more possibilities, if you try. After you've done your mantra for five to ten minutes, go into a silence and let your mind go blank. It is at this time that you become one with your higher self. You should be able to see a bright light thru your closed eyelids. Keep a pen and writing paper handy and write down your thots as they come to you. You can use this meditation technique to go to sleep. This may induce spiritual meaning into your dreams.

* * *

Your beliefs are based on personal experience. Your higher self emerges when you are inspired. Learn to separate good memories from bad ones. Learn the lessons contained in your bad memories. Then let them go. Substitute a good memory for the bad one. Forget and release the memories you don't want to keep.

* * *

Don't let your ego interfere with what you must do. It can affect the quality of your work and even undermine the success of your efforts. You can tell when your ego is disproportionate. It is normal to have some ego and say "I am this way or that way and that's a good way to be".

* * *

Don't let others rob you of your self-esteem. Your feeling of self-worth is very important to the success of your goals. If somebody tries to put you down or insults you, simply say "No thanks" and turn your back on them.

* * *

We are surrounded by currents of creativity that imbue us with creative ideas that you can use in your hobbies or in your career. While meditating ask for them to come to you and inspire you. Keep writing materials on hand and record ideas as they come to you.

* * *

In every endeavor take time to do things right. It will instill a sense of personal pride. There is no sense in doing things half-heartedly.

* * *

When you worry about things you can't control, you make things worse. Concentrate on a solution. Find ways over or around obstacles There's solution to every problem. You can try meditation to find the answer.

* * *

There are three steps to getting what you want. The first step is wanting or needing. Make certain that the thing you want is something that you will really use. Do you want this thing, so you can lord it over others? Better get your ego in check. Only ask for things that you have a strong and burning desire for. Things that will make your life better and easier.

Next, don't take no for an answer! If there are obstacles preventing you from attaining the thing or situation you desire—go around them! In some cases, you may have to develop a savings program and put off acquiring the specific thing you want until you can pay cash. Don't go into debt for something when there is no immediate need for it. Stairstep your goal; don't make the steps so large that you are likely to fail in their accomplishment. It is better to take many tiny steps than to falter and fail.

The final step is knowing/believing that you will accomplish your goal. Form a picture in your mind of you having or doing what you want. Hold that picture firmly in your mind for as long as you can. Then let it go feeling a great sense of satisfaction and accomplishment. This is called creative visualization.

* * *

Be happy with the little things life has to offer; and the big things will come! Each time you visualize strive for a feeling of gratitude. Be happy with the knowledge that what you ask for will manifest at some point in the future. When you create what you want with your mind it is called a thot form.

* * *

Don't listen to people with low expectations. By doing so, you are allowing them to limit your future.

* * *

Don't live in the past reminiscing in past laurels and failures. Live in the moment and create your future. Past bad circumstances can only dictate your present or future if you let them.

* * *

Some people aren't happy unless they want something. Don't get in the rut of keeping up with the Joneses. Only want what you can use. How much stuff do you have in the basement or in the garage that you never use and is just accumulating dust?

* * *

Don't build up your ego at the expense of others. Instead build up their egos by complimenting them and giving them praise when they do something right. You'll find out you wind up feeling better about yourself when you do so.

* * *

Learn to see that we are all connected by the light. Surround yourself with the bright light of protection. Turn your problems over to God/ the Light for resolution. Make a list of things you can do to alleviate the problem and then act on them. Do positive affirmations and then leave the rest up to God for completion.

* * *

We are the sum of the choices we make. Practice mind control to eliminate destructive thinking and behavior. Go on a negative diet and counter each negative thot with the statement "That's not true or that's not going to happen." Substitute a positive affirmation and say it three times. Let go of all negative ideas and thot patterns. Think about things that make that make you happy. Let go and let God!

* * *

The power of the mind is very impressive—if you think positive thots, positive things will come to you. Negative thots beget negative manifestations. Distance yourself from negative people and situations. Seek out relationships with happy positive people.

* * *

In as much as we are all connected to each other, it might help if we prayed for others. What I do is touch the light and say:' "God bless _____ may he/she have a wonderful life and many blessings". And in most cases, that's all I say. I also touch the light and send it to them.

* * *

It may not be possible to conjure love for people we consider enemies. But we can touch the light and send it to them. The value of this practice is two-fold: first, it sets up a field of protection around you. And secondly, it may soften the other person's attitude towards you. Remember the light is love.

God says; we have to love everybody but, we don't have to like them all.

* * *

Respect the opinions of others but, pick and choose what you want to accept. Embrace constructive criticism; make sure to evaluate it to make sure it's right. Reject ideas that encourage subscribing to status quo.

* * *

Respect the rights of others to be who they are. Compliment their personality traits that you find admirable. The more you promote goodwill, the happier you will be.

* * *

In getting away from stress, it is helpful to go for a walk and become one with nature. Look at the magnificent trees in all their majesty. Commune with the grass and pretty flowers. Embrace all of creation. You will feel at one with the universe. Because we are connected to everything.

* * *

Make a list of things about yourself that you want to improve and start today. If you lose today, you'll lose tomorrow. Never put things off to the next day because the next day never comes.

* * *

Our soul is the true essence of our being. If it is full of blotches—we suffer. Bask in the light to get rid of bad karma.

* * *

Radiate your enthusiasm—all fear vanishes when enthusiasm is present. Recover that childlike lust for life. Go into that quiet place in your mind. Find that childly happiness and apply it to your thot form—it becomes super charged and will manifest sooner.

* * *

Do the things you're afraid to do—things that most people take for granted. Don't put it off for days on end. This is fear of failure. Meditate before doing things that scare you. Think about the steps you'll take to accomplish the task before you. There's no such thing as failure. If it doesn't work the first time, think about what you did and learn from your mistakes—then try again.

* * *

Learn to appreciate your body. When you look in the mirror don't say: "I look older or I look younger than I did yesterday." Say instead: "I am eternally young.". As you know, your cells are constantly replacing themselves. Every seven years every cell in your body has been completely replaced. Instruct your body to replace the older cells with younger cells. Do this every day; there's no reason you can't get younger instead of older.

* * *

Laughter can heal the body and the soul. Watch comedy shows and think of things to laugh about every day and sooner or later, you'll see the difference in your demeanor. Think positive and visualize to effect the change.

* * *

Ask and you shall receive… as you think so shall it be.

* * *

Thot forms begin as a wish which evolves into a desire and gradually becomes an intention backed by a commitment and determination to see things thru. When you get to the point where you know that what you desire will come to pass, that's when things become manifest.

* * *

The road to hell is paved with good intentions. If you really plan to do something, do it now!

* * *

To some people the grass is always greener on the other side of the hill. Learn to be happy with what you have, and you will get more.

* * *

Once a wise man was traveling down the road and met a man who was going the other way. He said he was going to the city and asked what the people were like there. The wise man asked what the people were like where he came from. The traveler said they were all selfish, greedy and stingy. The wise man said the people in the city were the same. A while later the wise man met another stranger who said he was going to the city and wondered what the people were like. The wise man asked the stranger what the people were like where he came from. The stranger said they were all generous and wonderful people. The wise man said the people in the city were the same.

* * *

There is a field of energy which surrounds the body and manifests as colored lights. Doctors studying this multicolored aura can pinpoint disease in its early stages and cure it before it gets serious. This process was developed by Russian scientists and is called Kirlian photography.

* * *

We are spiritual beings having a material experience. Feed your soul as you would feed your body. Meditate every day and go for walks. Become one with nature. Work on your ability to contact your higher self. Do this thru meditation and by basking in the light.

* * *

We are all programed to a greater or lesser degree for better or worse. Seek to enhance the positive and eliminate the negative. This cannot be stressed enough! Refuse bad and limiting thots. Say: "I do not accept this kind of thinking—I am geared for success!".

* * *

Let go of all your thots. The positive for manifestation and the negative for elimination.

* * *

Live in the now. Do the things you've been putting off. Don't try to multi-task. Doing two or more things at the same time results in both jobs being poorly done or not finished. Remember to reward yourself once the task is finished.

* * *

We are encouraged to be average. Dare to rise above the norm.

* * *

Be grateful for the opportunity to work. Thank the light for a healthy body and for helping you to perform your tasks.

* * *

You can have eternal youth—don't embrace age fight it! When you look in the mirror, see yourself as you want to be. Drink lots of water and exercise. Use the positive affirmation" I am eternally young.".

* * *

In your interpersonal relationships put you before me. Become a people person.

* * *

Use positive affirmations to get rid of pain. Focus on the painful area and learn to relish it. The pain should go away. That's what members of the Special Forces do; when they are captured and tortured for information—they embrace the pain. Also, you can put the bright light on it and ask it to take the pain away.

* * *

We can't help but judge people when we meet them, But, set your prejudices aside and give them a chance. If they prove to be negative selfish people, get away from them and send the bright light of love to them. This gives you protection.

* * *

You get treated the way you teach people to treat you. Expect and demand respect. If they insult or mistreat you. Simply walk away and shield yourself with the bright light of protection.

* * *

You have within you a tremendous amount of potential. Go into a meditative state and think of things you like to do and are good at. Adopt those talents as hobbies. As you perfect your skills you may be able to make a living at it. You could start your own business.

* * *

At some point you may want to change jobs. Being happy with what you do is more important than money. When you like what do, you will get promotions faster.

* * *

Become aware of the potential of your friends and associates. Encourage them to cultivate their latent talents. Don't be surprised if their abilities are the same as yours. Maybe you can work on a project together.

Anyone can overcome limiting thoughts. Go into a meditative state and do positive affirmations. Dispel the damaging thoughts and tell them they no longer have power over you. Recognize your problems and take steps to alleviate them.

* * *

Anyone can attain a state of self-actualization. First put your house in order. Get rid of all negative limiting thots. Substitute positive ideas and imagine an ideal future for yourself. Set aside half an hour to an hour for meditation. Start an exercise program and pay attention to your diet. Start reading self-help books and take uo a hobby. Creativity helps feelings of anxiety and depression.

* * *

We are all so busy garnering wealth for material possessions that we forget to enjoy life. Take some of the money you have squirreled away and get away for the weekend.

* * *

Be an individual and lose the noose of conformity and the suit. Wear a sports jacket and a dress shirt and a pair of jeans (if you can get away with it). Don't seek to be a part of the status quo.

* * *

When you make decisions, don't pay attention to unsolicited advice. Ask yourself: "Is this what I really want?" Then take it from there.

* * *

Don't live in the past or the future. If you want to do something... do it now! Remember the lessons you've learned in the past and plan your goals for the future. Then come back to the present. LIVE IN THE NOW!

* * *

Almost all of us have some form of paranoia. This leads to conjuring other fears and before we know it, we're a bundle of nerves. Go into a meditative state and examine when you first became afraid that something bad could happen. Dismiss the idea and say: "I am loved, and nothing can harm me." Repeat this phrase as many times as you feel is necessary.

* * *

You have the option to change your thinking. Remember that negative thots beget more negative thots and positive thots attract more positive thots. Positive thinking reduces stress and anxiety. There's no better time to do it than today.

* * *

It doesn't hurt to have role models. But stay away from hero worship. If your hero is a drug addict, alcoholic or over indulges in sex. It's time to evaluate your standing as a human being.

* * *

You can attain higher levels of functioning—if you break away from the mean. There is nothing admirable about being mediocre. Make a list of worthwhile goals and make a commitment to achieve them one at a time Get away from limited thinking habits and aspire to succeed.

* * *

Learn to think for yourself. Stop listening to people who think they know what's best for you. There's no point in wallowing in mediocrity when you can soar like an eagle.

* * *

You are responsible for the thots you have. Self-defeating attitudes are the result of negative thinking. So, change your thinking.

* * *

The more we limit ourselves thru negative thinking—the more we limit our potential for success.

* * *

What is it like to be actualized? Functioning at a higher level—you'll see opportunity everywhere, you'll see possibilities for growth in everything. You'll see beauty in little things. Every day presents new adventures. You'll feel at one with all creation. You'll be satisfied with every aspect of life. You'll feel love without expectation. You'll accept others for who they are and don't put others down for their beliefs. Your feeling of oneness will leave you feeling at peace with the universe. You'll want to help others feel as you do. You'll recognize everyone as individuals unique unto themselves. When you are actualized you don't feel anxiety stress or depression. You are unafraid of life. You don't feel unworthy of the good things life has to offer. You won't allow the opinions of others to affect your way of doing things. You'll create your own destiny and do not accept judgements. You listen to constructive criticism but, will not let destructive criticism sway you from attaining your goals. You readily adapt to circumstances when it's called for. You speak your mind freely—but are always concerned with the feelings of others. You stairstep your goals so as not to overextend yourself. You'll never lord who you are, what you've accomplished or what you have over others. Self-actualized people get their inspirations both from within and the world around them. At the end of the day they look back at their activities and decide what they did right and what they can do better.

* * *

Deep within all of us is hidden a little child who needs your attention. Bring it to the surface and pay attention to its needs. Take him/her for a walk and commune with nature. Buy it an ice cream or a chocolate bar. Laugh at silly jokes, play games, watch a cartoon or a kid's movie. Remember that deep down inside we're all still little. Pay attention to the child's needs and you'll be happier.

* * *

There are four steps to teaching: first tell them what you're going to tell them; then tell them; then tell them what you told them; then have them tell you what you told them. When you're talking to people you have to tell them twice. The first time it goes in one ear and out the other; the second time it sinks in.

* * *

Insecurity is often fear of failure. Close your eyes and look up and see the bright light of God. Then think about how you're going to take step by step to do the thing you plan on doing. Then relax let go and let God.

* * *

When your body's sick your mind needs rest. When your mind is sick it can manifest a physical illness. All you can do is go into a meditative state and correct the problem by using positive affirmations.

* * *

Approach work as play and tell yourself how much you are going to enjoy it. Envision the job as complete and well done. If it's worth doing, it's worth doing right.

* * *

When you hate someone, it degenerates the soul. Develop a complacent attitude toward that person. Tell yourself that you don't care about that person one way or the other. At this point, you should be able to send him/her the bright light (the light is love). In two easy steps it may be possible to turn an enemy into a friend.

* * *

Keep an open mind about confusing issues. Look for a third alternative where both sides are satisfied.

* * *

Swearing depreciates both the speaker and the listener.

* * *

When you're tired, drink a glass of water and go into a meditative state for fifteen or twenty minutes. You should come out of it feeling refreshed.

* * *

Try to drink eight glasses of water a day. If you want to gain weight drink lots of water.

If you want to lose weight, drink lots of water. Remember we're supposed to be eighty per cent water. Water will help purge illness and disease.

* * *

If you want to counteract aging, increase your blood circulation and feel better in general adopt a modest exercise program that includes stretching.

* * *

If you want to quit smoking. It's not hard to do. Write out your reasons on a file card and carry It with you. Every time you feel the need to smoke, read your card; and remind yourself why you want to quit. Set a date when you want to quit. Then just to it. However, if you don't create an image of yourself as nonsmoker you'll start again.

* * *

Your favorite fantasies eventually evolve into thot forms. Sooner or later they will become manifest. As you think so shall it be.

* * *

There is no such thing as failure. Learn from your mistakes and try again. Keep trying until you get it right.

* * *

It is in dying that we are born into eternal light.

* * *

Before you do anything, think things thru and put the bright light of God on it. Let go and let God. Then go about your business with the knowledge that you will do your best.

* * *

If your marriage is on the rocks and it looks like your headed for divorce. Give your marriage a ninety-day probation. Here are the ground rules: First get counseling Then:.

1) The wife gets up with the husband. Have coffee together. Don't read the newspaper. Have a polite conversation.
2) Wife should get a part-time job (if she isn't already working.)
3) Wife should put on makeup, fix her hair and make sure she's dressed decent.
4) When the husband gets home from work; after he's wound down from traffic. He should do chores around the house (empty trash, fold laundry etc.).
5) Prepare dinner and do dishes together.
6) Spend two hours together talking or watching television.
7) Go out on a date at least one night a week.
8) On Sundays go out on a family outing.

If at the end of ninety days, you're still not getting along, The husband should move out and get an apartment. The wife should get a full-time job. They should figure out expenses and agree on support. The husband should take the kids one night a week and at least every other weekend.

If at the end of six months, if you still want a divorce… go ahead. It would be great if you could remain friends and say to each other: "I'll help you find your path and you can help me find my path.

* * *

No matter how you look at it, abortion is murder! It should only be allowed in the case of rape or incest or for medical reasons.

There are many prospective parents out there and many of them are unable to get a baby.

If you are pregnant and are unable to keep the baby, go to an adoption agency and tell them you want: all doctor, medical bills and hospital expenses paid for. Also, the cost of maternity clothes should be paid for. You should also ask for full living expenses for the last three months of the pregnancy and for one-month convalescence after the baby is born. In addition, you should ask for a spending allowance for the last four months (fifty dollars week would be fair.).

It should be noted that there are plenty of older kids out there who would love to have a home and a family.

* * *

There is something to be said for fidelity and celibacy. If you're having a problem with promiscuity and would like to change, see a clergyman or a psychiatrist.

* * *

Your worth as a person comes from within. Personal possessions do not define you. You are not your house or your car. God wants you to have the best of everything. As long as your possessions do not possess you. And, you do not lord what you have over others.

* * *

It might be time to make a list of things that bother you. Make plans to rectify them. Start with the little things first and work your way up. Don't let trivial things affect your mood; or get in the way of your relationships.

* * *

Channel your creative urges. Every good boy/girl deserves a hobby. Sometimes your pass-times can develop into a part time income. It is important to have a diversion. It can have a positive effect on depression and anxiety.

* * *

Trust your inner-self when making plans and decisions. Go into a meditative state and relax. Say to your higher self: "I have a problem I think you can help me with. I need to know about this or that. Be still and know the answer will come to you.

* * *

You may be fooling yourself about a certain thing, and you know you're doing it. The more you lie to yourself; the more self-contempt you'll create. If you can't be honest with yourself –how can you expect to be honest with others?

* * *

Say to yourself: "I was born to cultivate all the creative potential within me.".

* * *

Don't compromise what you believe in. Don't let the opinions of others affect your decision to do what's right. Other people want you to be mediocre. Don't let others bring you down. Think independently – break away from the status quo and soar like an eagle.

* * *

If you're in a rut, the best thing you can do is take a day off and do something fun. The child within you know what to do.

* * *

You have the potential for happiness. Purge all negative thots and substitute positive affirmations. Get back to nature and buy the child within a soda pop.

* * *

When our higher needs are cut off (a sense of belonging, individuality or love and affection). We tend to become anxious or depressed. Make a list of your priorities and work thru the list from the smallest to the big ones. Don't hesitate to add to the list as ideas come to you.

* * *

Telling the truth is easier than telling a lie. If you lie, you wind up telling more lies to back up the first one. Pretty soon you'll forget what you said and get caught.

* * *

Self-renewal, recreation and creativity are important to your well-being. Don't hesitate to take time for these things.

* * *

Beauty is only skin deep—so they say. But, it is important to keep yourself looking good. Don't skimp on buying clothes, makeup and hair dye. You should meet and fill your inner needs. Self-esteem should be at the top of your list.

* * *

We should have a sense of purpose to fill the void that might otherwise be there. Maybe—one day a month—you might get involved in some type of charitable work. Or be an assistant coach for a little league team. Maybe you can visit a terminally ill patient or an elderly person.

* * *

You can only reach your full potential by taking one tiny step at a time. You can manifest change in your life by doing so. Remember your oneness with all the universe. Be kind to others. Become one with your goals. Don't accept evil or negative things in your life. Avoid negative people and situations. Be excited and enthusiastic about your life. Do things to make your life worthwhile. Demand and expect good things in your life and they will come to you.

* * *

Obliterate bad memories from your mind and learn the lessons that are contained there. Let go and let God. Look for slow growth day by day and eventually you will attain your goals.

* * *

Erase bad feelings, thots and emotions and replace them with positive affirmations. Exist at a higher level, strive to become full and complete within yourself, and you will establish a sense of well-being. Don't settle for less than your best. Don't fall prey to stereotypes of age, gender, race, color or creed. The self-directed person doesn't subscribe to labels. Be a winner but not at the expense of others. Don't compete with others, compete with yourself. Learn from your mistakes and go forward.

* * *

Be at peace with yourself. Purge all negative thots and fill your mind with happy thots. If life hands you a lemon… make lemonade. Our thots affect our emotions and our health. It is possible to groom your thinking and only have positive thots. Remember like attracts like.

* * *

See yourself as a winner—we can all be winners in the game of life. Affirm your oneness with all creation. In all eternity there is only one.

* * *

When the student is ready the master will appear. Sometimes from within and sometimes in the form of another person. The divine force of the universe is within you. Be still and know.

* * *

Every action begins with a thot. Go into a meditative state and think things thru. We are only limited by the laws of nature and time. Leave behind old limiting thot patterns and tell yourself: "I will succeed.". Jesus said: "Anything I can do, you can do and more.".

* * *

In one sense, reality as we perceive it, is a figment of our imagination—in that we create our own realities. The only true reality is thot. Man has a non-material consciousness capable of influencing matter. You have the capacity to create miracles and influence your state of affairs. You can find proof of this by reflecting on personal experience. Use positive affirmations daily.

* * *

Self-empowerment means to promote self-actualization—which means to realize ones full potential.

* * *

Anything your mind can conceive can be manifest.

* * *

Don't handicap yourself with ideas of limitation. Think in terms of abundance. See it first in your mind, then make it happen. Use the power of prayer (affirmations).

* * *

I am here to be the best I can be.

* * *

Desires, wishes, hopes and fantasies are the beginnings of manifestation. Because they evolve into thot forms.

* * *

Accept others for who they are. Give them the respect they deserve.

* * *

Expectation and enthusiasm will bring your thot form to fruition.

* * *

We are all spiritual beings having a physical experience. Learn the lessons life has to offer. We need to understand to be understood.

* * *

God has no form… God is everywhere.

* * *

A good relationship does not mean giving up what you want, in consideration for the other person. Seek a compromise—that way you both win!

You created all that resides within you. Albeit, we were programmed when we were little. But subscribing to old beliefs is up to us. You control your thinking.

* * *

See God in everyone you meet.

* * *

Discord can't exist if you don't participate.

* * *

All things are possible for those who love God.

* * *

You deserve prosperity. God wants you to prosper. When you have what you need and what you want. Don't forget that there are charities out there that need your help.

* * *

In changing your inner beliefs, catch all negative thots and replace them with positive affirmations.

* * *

Never say: "I'll do it tomorrow". Because tomorrow never comes.

* * *

Strive for what you want. Become one with what you're doing. Meditate before you act. Spiritual prosperity is within you. All you have to do is bring it out. If you can believe it –you can create it.

* * *

The idea that you can't change is a misconception and a crutch. All you have to do is do it!

* * *

As you think, so shall it be… you are as you think.

* * *

Emotions are manifestations of thot. Think happy thots and be enthusiastic.

* * *

Think about what you want—not about what you don't want. Thots can create miracles. Miracles happen when you purge the concept of impossibilities and believe in possibilities.

* * *

The soul is one with the universe.

* * *

Replace doubt with a knowing that things will work out. Maybe not according to your plans but, according to divine plan.

* * *

Create a healthy body, watch your diet and exercise.

* * *

Your status in life reflects your state of mind.

* * *

There is a continuum—you can call it cosmic consciousness.

* * *

Your thots affect those around you. If you're feeling down don't be surprised if they express gloomy thots. If your mood is up watch those around you light up.

* * *

Your thots create your reality. Be careful what you think.

* * *

Write your representatives when a condition upsets you. And give them a phone call. Send them a copy of your letter every month.

* * *

Radiate your feelings of love and others will pick it up.

* * *

Learn to love yourself—first, last, and foremost. Give yourself a hug and tell yourself "I love you.".

* * *

Plato is an interesting read, albeit a bit tedious. Here are a few things he said:

Plato equated the mind with the soul.

God/good once seen must be inferred that it is the cause of all things good and beautiful.

The soul came down from the light above.

The power of knowledge is present in the soul of each person.

A weak nature will never be responsible for great things.

Our soul is immortal and never perishes.

Good preserves and benefits the soul.

The soul is worth more than the body.

Death is a migration of the soul from one place to another.

* * *

Many are called but few are chosen. To be chosen, one must first choose to be chosen. Your soul must be free of blight.

* * *

Ask and you shall receive.

* * *

We create much of our own suffering.

* * *

Being obstinate and having to have your own way will get you nowhere.

* * *

Don't try to be what other people want you to be. Be loyal to yourself.

* * *

Live in the now. You can't change the past. You can plan the future, but you can't do anything about it till it happens. Live in the now!

* * *

Worrying about things that could happen can make them happen. Give yourself credit for being able to solve problems as they come up.

* * *

Don't waste your time pursuing goals that other people want you to accomplish. Your priorities should be number one.

* * *

Live in the present moment.

* * *

Be grateful for what you have and for what you will receive.

* * *

Your consciousness can become one with universal mind thru meditation.

* * *

Place yourself in service to others by doing little things and sharing the light.

* * *

What does meditation do for you? Meditation reduces stress; rejuvenates the brain and increases its' effectiveness. Meditation reduces depression, anxiety and panic attacks. It stays off degeneration of the brain; improves mental disorders; helps reduce addiction; enhances happiness;

bolsters self-esteem and gives you a sense of well-being. Meditation boosts optimism and helps control negative emotions.

* * *

When doing thot forms always adopt a feeling of gratitude. Always give thanks when you pray.

* * *

Bless and release all things and all monies (things lost or stolen) no longer in your possession. Say: "What is meant for me will come to me,".

* * *

When you have a disagreement… compromise. There's always a third alternative; that will leave you both happy.

* * *

Bless your enemies and send them the bright Light of God (the light is love). Shield yourself with the bright Light of protection.

* * *

Change your thinking habits from disbelief to belief. Bring things into the realm of possibility. Your thinking does not control you, you control your thinking.

* * *

Why worry when you can pray? It releases the latent powers God has given you. It stimulates your thinking.

* * *

There is an advantage for every disadvantage. Take the problem and tear it to pieces. Examine every piece of the puzzle. You will find things that can be exploited. Put yourself in God's hands. Trust the light to get you thru the problem. Every problem is an opportunity.

* * *

Every day, in every way I get better and better.

* * *

Everything in the universe is energy vibrating at various frequencies. You have the power to raise your frequency; and eliminate any problems. Energy can neither be created nor destroyed. It merely changes frequencies. You can adjust lower frequency vibrations to higher ones; simply by willing it. Go into a meditative state and tell your higher self to raise the frequency—it's as simple as that!

* * *

Allow others to be right occasionally—it satiates their ego.

* * *

An abundance of everything is available to you. All you must do is ask repeatedly; knowing that your prayers will be answered. You must have a burning desire that can't be extinguished, to achieve your goals.

* * *

When it comes to criticism coming from others; don't take it personally. Forgive them and let it go. Surround yourself with the bright light of protection. Do what you think is right.

* * *

Radiate happiness—it wards off discontent and depression. Coupled with enthusiasm—you become a human dynamo.

* * *

We can all feel the presence of God during meditation.

* * *

God/the Light resides not in the past or the future but in the eternal now.

* * *

Once you realize that Divine Love does exist. You can direct it to your needs, wants and desires. Just be certain that what you ask for will bring no harm to others and will benefit others beside yourself.

* * *

Replace, your fears with love from God/the Light. Know that nothing can harm you; for God's love is omnipotent.

* * *

We are not separate from God/the Light, who dwells within our soul. God/the Light is not available to some people and not to others. The Divine Light is available to everybody.

* * *

With God/the Light all things are possible.

* * *

God/the Light will not reside where there is evil. Nor will the spiritual aspect of your soul.

* * *

God is the Light. The Light is Love. It is available to you at any time. When you have a problem, send the Light. Love never fails.

* * *

When you have a problem, put the bright Light of Love on it—love never fails. When faced with a problem assert your faith in form of positive affirmations and touch the light. You will create a field of energy that will inspire you. The answer to the problem will come to you. Turn your problems over to God/the Light and you will receive an answer.

* * *

You have the power to heal yourself. Put the bright Light upon the afflicted area and talk to your body and encourage it to heal. Purge your mind of all negative feelings and forgive yourself for any transgressions. Ask God /the Light to heal you.

* * *

We are not separate from God/the Light. You would have no fear if you believe that the Light is expressing Itself thru you. Fear and God can't dwell in you at the same time.

* * *

When faced with a problem, assert your faith in form of positive affirmations and touch the Light. You'll create a field of energy that will inspire you. The answer to your problem will come to you. Turn your problems over to God/the Light and you will receive an answer.

* * *

Pray for those who are suffering. Send them the Light. Remember we are all connected.

* * *

Light vibrates at a higher rate. Focus the Light on all your problems; and they will begin to dissolve. Use the Light for protection and healing.

* * *

By generating the Light around you can affect those in contact with you, in a positive way.

* * *

Counter dark thots by contemplating the Light and use positive affirmations.

* * *

Spread joy where ever you go. This will make you are a sought-after person.

* * *

God/the Light best and most often declares itself from within us.

* * *

There is goodness in material wealth. God/the Light wants us to enjoy its bounty. As long as we don't allow material things to possess us. Don't let worldly things. distract you from God/the Light or each other. Give God/the Light credit for what you have. It would be admirable if you could give something to charity.

* * *

Attitudes are more important than facts. If you're down on your luck and the wolf is at the door. Remember God/the Light is with you helping and guiding you. Fill your mind with thots of confidence. Form a picture of yourself succeeding. Cancel all negative thoughts and counter them with positive affirmations. Develop a wholesome self-respect. Believe that you receive the power of God/the Light; for the kingdom of God is within you. Empty your thots of all negative thinking and substitute positive happy thots.

* * *

Keep your conversations happy and positive. Avoid negative statements.

* * *

We can consciously tap into an unlimited source of power. The power of the Light, the power of God.

* * *

When in contact with the Light, thru our thots—we acquire unlimited power. When mind body and spirit work together in harmony with one another; we receive all the energy we need to accomplish the tasks that lie before us.

* * *

Within the mind are all the resources we need for successful living. The Light gives us all the power we need to do so. It is up to us to contact and use those powers.

* * *

When you pray don't say please; say thank you. Knowing that your prayers have been heard and answered.

* * *

Results do not manifest for people who don't give themselves to the desired results. Whatever you're doing give it two hundred percent.

If you want a thing or situation with all your heart—it will come to fruition. What the mind anticipates will become a reality. What the mind really wants, it will receive. The power of faith works wonders. There is no obstacle you can't beat!

* * *

You can do all things with the Light which strengthens you. With help from the Light… you can do anything!

* * *

As you think… so shall it be.

* * *

Worry and fear thots limit the flow of energy. Empty these thots from your mind, with the statement: "All fear, worry and anxiety are leaving me now with help from the Light." Now fill the empty space with positive affirmations.

* * *

Make the Light your partner in everything you do.

* * *

For every problem, there is a solution, keep calm; being uptight blocks the flow of spiritual power. Go into a meditative state and wait for a solution.

* * *

Anger and hate have a powerful effect on your physical and mental health. To heal yourself you must first purge all feelings of anger and resentment and fill your mind with happy and positive thots. Go into a meditative state and say to yourself: "The Light is now giving me a healthy body and _____ (put in any specific request).

* * *

Like your work and it will become easier. Plan your work—don't get in a hurry. Develop a positive attitude. Think of your job as easy and it will become easy. Don't multi-task. Don't put off till tomorrow what you can do today. Pray and ask the Light to help you. It will make your work simpler.

* * *

Learn to like people—get to know them and give them compliments— you'll feel better for it. We all like to have lots of friends. All things are possible for those who love God.

* * *

Sin is a mistake to be corrected, not an evil to be punished.

* * *

Miracles occur naturally as expressions of love. The real miracle is the love that inspires them.

* * *

There is no such thing as time in the afterlife. There is only now.

* * *

Lack cannot exist, when you are completely in the Light.

* * *

Judging others does not define them—it defines you. Send others unconditional love/the Light.

* * *

Avoid tribal labels—find out who you really are.

* * *

Don't blame others or situations for your present circumstances. Think back and you will see where you made mistakes that put you where you are.

* * *

Anything your mind can conceive can be manifest in your reality.

* * *

Your physical body and the material world are not in the true sense reality. They are only temporary. Open your mind to the possibilities of other realities being available to you.

* * *

When you are relaxed, you can become inspired. The more efficient and productive you become. Enjoy the moment and more will come.

* * *

Doubt limits your perspective and restricts your potential to be your best.

* * *

Your thots create your reality.

* * *

God/the Light does not plan for you to suffer. Look for the benefits and lessons to be learned from your pain.

* * *

The judgement of others is irrelevant. If they're right, you will know it from within. If they're wrong, reject their criticism and protect yourself with the Light.

* * *

Faith is an energy that dwells within you at all times.

* * *

Take an impartial perspective when dealing with situations. Leave your ego out of it.

* * *

All things are possible for those who love God.

* * *

You don't need to prove yourself better than others. Think of yourself as being special and those around you as being special too. Remember we're all connected. We all can be extra special. The Light has no favorites—we are all special where God is concerned. See yourself connected to the Light and the Universe. You are an extension of the Light.

* * *

Good listeners earn the reputation of being good conversationalists.

* * *

Every day in every way, I get better and better.

* * *

In a meditative state ask your higher self to show you the way. And it will be shown to you.

* * *

Give what you can, if you don't have anything to give –give your time and attention.

* * *

Every aspect of your life takes place in the now—not the past or the future.

* * *

There's an answer for every problem. Do your breathing and your affirmations. be still and know. The answer will come to you.

* * *

If God were to take human form—I'd like to think she'd be a woman. Because, women are more nurturing and more forgiving.

* * *

The Light is here for all of us. There is not a separate God for each of us. We are each an individualized expression of the Lght.

* * *

You can be addicted to almost anything. When you are addicted you want more, more, more.

* * *

We carry our attributes and our shortcomings over to the next life.

* * *

We are all of the same essence. We are all made from the Light.

* * *

Hatred, envy, anger, anxiety and negative thots can block us from using our inner power.

* * *

The best way to over-come fear of failure is… just do it.

* * *

Peace of mind is essential in accessing your inner power.

* * *

Relaxation is critical for the body and the mind. When you are tense—you can't do things right. Tension can cause physical problems as well.

* * *

If you believe God is for you. Tremendous power is available to you. Who can be against you?

* * *

When you pray—you align yourself with the Light.

* * *

Try to do your best in everything you do. Don't compete with others. Don't try to impress anyone. Perfect your skills to get better and better.

* * *

Given the power of God/the Light, we can accomplish all our goals.

* * *

For every disadvantage there is an advantage. Go into a meditative state; and roll the problem over in your mind. An answer will come to you.

* * *

The power of belief makes a big difference.

* * *

Good outcomes are not diminished by intelligent thinking. Rather it reduces problems and gets positive results.

* * *

God's peace and understanding is in my mind and body now. I am not alone. The Light is with me always. God/the Light will help me in all my decisions. I am being helped and I will act on it.

* * *

Thots externalize into actualization.

* * *

At our center the Light has placed a remarkable soul. It can do wonderous things and to know God.

* * *

Hope and faith gives us enthusiasm, vibrancy and vitality.

* * *

We tend to become one with what we imagine or visualize.

* * *

Long life can result from the quality of thots we think.

* * *

Intense desire leads to the manifestation of that which is sought after.

* * *

First and foremost, learn to forgive yourself for the mistakes you've made. Learn the lessons contained there.

* * *

It's all right to cry—tears cleanse the soul.

* * *

Energy can neither be created nor destroyed. If our soul is energy—it makes a good case for an after-life.

* * *

We are one with nature, thru our connection with Divine Mind.

* * *

Mind is the source of all power. We all vary in the amount of power we use. We are all tied to that source of power. We might call it Universal Mind. We are all individualized vehicles of expression for that Mind.

All are one in Universal Mind. In our experience, we can use that power consciously or subconsciously.

* * *

Know what you want and don't hesitate to ask for it. Know that you are worthy and that others will benefit as well.

* * *

Always give thanks when doing thot forms. This affirms your belief that you will get what you ask for.

* * *

The power of the Light is available always—to those who seek it.

* * *

Thinking in terms of want creates a condition of poverty. Thinking in terms of opulence begets prosperity.

* * *

You have your future within you. Think positive happy thots.

* * *

Spiritual growth is a rewarding and exciting process. Meditate at least once a day.

* * *

Making believe that the future will be the same as the past; gears us for failure. You have the experience to do better—even if it is the same.

* * *

It is easy to dismiss what we know and submit to the opinions of other people. If you have a mentor, who gives you good solid advice. Listen to him/her. On the other hand, evaluate and re-evaluate what others tell you. If it's good advice—embrace it. If it's not—forget it. Many people see nothing wrong with mediocrity. Don't let those people drag you down to their level.

* * *

Knowing is the key to building successful thot-forms. Know that sooner or later, what you visualize will become manifest. Then visualize the thing or situation, you desire; as often as you can every day. Eventually it will come to fruition.

* * *

No one knows you better than you know yourself. You—not someone else—must make critical decisions about your life. Your reactions to situations are more important than the situations themselves. You have more control over your reactions than you do about the conditions.

* * *

Your life's experience is the best teacher you'll ever have. Do you have something going on right now; that is like something that happened in the past?

* * *

You and you alone are responsible for your happiness. You will also affect those around you with your moods. Negative emotions cannot exist when you have a happy attitude. Happiness is a positive cure-all for all negative feelings. You can bring happiness to those in close association with you. Focus on positive things rather than the negative.

* * *

Give credit to the insights of other people. It gives you a better perspective to what you're doing; and it makes them feel better about themselves.

* * *

See what you want and then make it happen. Focus on the oneness of everything, not the separateness. Life can only take place in the now.

* * *

Practice your breathing before you meditate. As you inhale feel yourself connecting with the Light. As you exhale feel your oneness with the world around you.

* * *

Mistakes are going to happen. You can learn from the experience. Go into the past and garner the knowledge to be had from the old goof-ups. Then release the bad memory from your mind—never to come back again.

* * *

Resolve conflicts in a win/win fashion. No one has to lose for the other to win. There's always a third alternative—where both parties come out winners.

* * *

Don't seek the approval of others. Self-approval is what's important.

* * *

Live in the present moment—not the past or the future. Develop an appreciation for the now of your existence. Seize and enjoy every moment. If you don't, you'll never be able to recover the time you lost. You can choose to have an effective life.

* * *

You teach others how to treat you. People can pick up your thots of low self-esteem as well as your body language—do your shoulders droop, do you hang your head, do you shuffle your feet when your walk? These things indicate that you have a loser's attitude and you will be treated accordingly. People pickup on those things.

* * *

To do anything, we must first believe that it can be accomplished. It paves the way to creative solutions. Lay out the stepping stones to reach your goal. Eliminate the word impossible from your vocabulary.

* * *

Make time every day for your kids and spouse. Make every Sunday family day.

* * *

Our material bodies reflect our spiritual life force. Practice good personal hygiene and exercise every day.

* * *

Good thots and ideas are no better than good dreams unless they are acted upon. Don't put off until tomorrow what you can today.

* * *

Your life is what your thots make it. As you think so you are. What we are is the result of our thinking. What we think, we become.

* * *

Create pictures in your mind of what you want to manifest in your life. Turn on your positive emotions so you can feel it. Use your feelings to emphasize the pictures in your mind.

* * *

An obstacle between you and what you want can be the lack of support from others. If they discourage you… turn your back on them.

* * *

You get out of life what you give. That's the basic concept of Karma. If you do good positive things in this life, you'll get positive things back, and vice versa. Sometimes you get immediate feedback and sometimes it doesn't come until your next life. But, one way or another you shall reap what you sow.

* * *

How do you get rid of bad Karma? By making certain everything you think say and do is positive and by...

Celebrating the Light: Stand with your feet splayed about a foot apart and raise your hands up to the Heavens and say: I am one with God and the universe. I am one with the Light. I am in the Light and the Light is within me; we are truly one.". Now bring your hands down cross your arms and say: "I am surrounded by the bright Light of protection and nothing can harm me.". Place your hands on your shoulders give yourself a hug and say: "For I am truly loved.". Raise your hands back up and say: "I rejoice and celebrate the life I've been given and all the blessings I receive: Eternal health, eternal youth, eternal wealth and eternal life and _____ (fill in specific requests.). I have the power indeed I am the power and I choose to share with universe.". Do this upon arising and before retiring and as many times during the day as you feel like doing it.

* * *

Go about your daily routines with the knowledge that things are working out for you. Remember that God is the Light and the Light is God and the Light is Love. That's what it's all about!

* * *

The last four letters of American are: I CAN.

* * *

Don' let bad memories from the past haunt you. Just remember the lessons you learned from them. Focus on the now and the future.

* * *

Non-existence means exactly that—you are not, never have been and never will be. I can't imagine any existence so bad that anyone would wish for that, at the end of their life. But if that's what the individual wants; I suppose it's possible.

Many people believe that there is just one life and nothing after. But that is just speculation and has nothing to do with reality.

Most Muslims, Christians and Jews believe in the concept of heaven and hell. Where we get our just rewards or punishment and spend the rest of eternity there.

Reincarnation is multifaceted. In its purest form we incarnate in three dimensions: past, present and future. Always on the same planet and in the same lifeform. Broader aspects of reincarnation would allow us to incarnate in varied lifeforms as reward or punishment based on the quality of this life.

In each life we must begin again. Garnering wealth and experience as we go; and losing it all when we die. Only to begin all over again. It is a shame that we that we do not accumulate enough wealth to live comfortably until late in life. At which point, when we have the time and money to do the things we've always wanted to do. But, our aged bodies prevent us from doing many things we didn't have time or money to do earlier in life.

* * *

Most of us live from paycheck to paycheck. We are still slaves to the almighty dollar. We earn enough to make mortgage payments, car payments and cover the necessities to get by from month to month. There may be a few embellishments to keep us happy; and a television set to keep us complacent; and daydreams of a better tomorrow that never comes.

* * *

We do have the ability to realize our potential the same way we do our thot forms. Focus on a picture. And hold it constant in your mind for as long as possible. Do it often every day without stopping or giving up. Never doubt the possibilities. Eventually you will realize the reality you deserve and desire. (realize: to bring from potential into actualization).

* * *

We all need someone to encourage us. Can you guess who is our greatest motivator? Look in the mirror… there he/she is. Give yourself a smile and say: "I can and I'm going to!" There's no better time to start than today!

* * *

The best way to do a thoughtform is: Formulate a picture of you doing exactly what you want to do. Or, having what you want and using the object of your desire. Hold the picture firmly in your mind. And release it into the atmosphere for manifestation. Do this as often as you can. Sooner or later you'll see the stepping stones you need to take to realize your goal.

* * *

Each one of us has tremendous potential. If we take a moment to budget our time and allocate just an hour a day to do something constructive and creative; that is in keeping with our goals and aspirations. We can accomplish great things.

* * *

One of the things the holds us back is lack of money. Work out a budget and see where your money is going. How much money do you spend on frivolous things for instant gratification? Is there a way this money can be better invested?

* * *

Do you have valuable possession lying around the house, that you never use and haven't used in years? Why not sell them and raise some money for your projects?

*　*　*

We could all use an ally to accomplish our goals. The first possibility is obvious—the most eligible person would be your spouse or lover. Or, maybe a friend or family member who shares a common interest.

*　*　*

Mind, consciousness and intellect are other terms used to describe the material aspect of our soul. It leaves our body upon death and becomes one with the spiritual aspect of our soul. The physical aspect of our soul is discernable by a speck of light reflected in our eyes, which disappears upon death. Have you ever heard the expression: "The eyes are the windows of the soul"?

*　*　*

Close your eyes and look straight up. You should see an intense silvery light. That is the spiritual aspect of your soul. Now, with your eyes closed, look in the direction of your forehead. You will see a silvery white light only not as bright. That is the physical aspect of your soul.

Negative thots, emotions and bad Karma can leave dark spots on the physical aspect of your soul. Too many blotches would preclude the physical aspect of your soul from communing with the spiritual aspect of your soul. Which should be our goal: both aspects in communion with one another. This is necessary for reincarnation. Under these circumstances a purgation s necessary. So, we don't take the bad Karma into our next life. How easy or difficult this will be being contingent upon our desire to be good. It can be accomplished thru meditation and celebrating the Light.

In some cases, our consciousness, may not want to dispel the blotches. If this is the case… we may have another Hitler on our hands.

*　*　*

If both aspects of our soul are not cohabiting our body. The spiritual aspect is directly above our head.

* * *

Once when I was driving from Phoenix to Denver; I parked the car and walked out into the desert. The hot July sun blinded me, and I sat on a rock to recover my vision. I heard a voice that said: "There is only one there is only now.". I drove myself crazy for a week to ten days trying to figure out the riddle.

Finally, I decided to take the words at face value. There is only one—everything in the universe is connected. There is only now—the past has passed and there is nothing we can do to change it. The future is uncertain and all we can do is prepare for it—that is done in the now. That is all there is to it… there is only one, there is only now.

* * *

There is a rumor that God went to sleep, and evil came into existence, because God wasn't watching. God never sleeps and allows evil to exist for the sake of balance.

* * *

Everything that exists, does so because God perceives it to exist.

* * *

We all create our own nightmares. All too often, others suffer because of our misconceptions. Now it's time to put your foot down and say: "I've had enough and I'm not going to take any more. And, I'm not going to back down.". Then ask the Light and the universe to help you and give you protection from evil. Remember to celebrate the Light every day.

* * *

Without evil, good would have no real definition. What is hot without cold? What is light without darkness? Beauty without ugliness and so on and so forth. We must put limits on things or there is no reason.

47

But, all of this is but one aspect of the issue between good and evil. We are the ones who set limits between good and evil, in our realities. Un-fortunately there is an overlap between our reality and those of others. There-in lies the danger.

If our imagined good is in dominion of our image of evil. And that concept is in concert with universal mind. Then the universe is predominantly good. And, we are safe. At least until tomorrow, when we must recreate our vison of benevolence.

* * *

Our disposition to do good in this life is contingent upon our ability to share our resources (time and money). If we have little to spare, then give that which has no limits: our happiness, positive and pure thots. Those things are much more valuable than gold, minutes and seconds.

* * *

An atheist's prayers are always answered.

* * *

Being a beggar sitting in front of a church begging for alms is the epitome of humility. Maybe, that's what we need to do. Disrobe ourselves of our self-centered concentration on our worldly goods and aspirations. And, focus our interests on the needs of others and upon achievements that benefit the many instead of the one. Which is –indeed—how we become one with the universe.

* * *

I like to imagine that my reason for being here is to realize my fantasies one at a time. If they benefit others besides myself; and bring no detriment to anyone.

* * *

Evil will always be subordinate to the good. It can exist for reasons already stated. The light has something to offer everybody. Evil can probably set a planet back to the stone age—but, cannot eliminate human life. Man-kinds survival is directly contingent upon the omnipotence of the Light. That the Light Is good is evidence by the order of the universe.

* * *

Can we really communicate with the Light? We must shed our ego, disappointments and feelings of un-worthiness; and appear before our maker completely transparent. We must be filled with positive anticipation and feel our oneness with the Light.

* * *

The world is full of winners and losers. In my opinion the winners are those who are happy with little things and consider themselves blessed and say: "This is as good as it gets.". The people who are happy with less than nothing; are the ones who deserve the most of everything.

* * *

We are not simply beings made of flesh and blood but are made of sub-atomic particles which manifest as flashes of light. They are called neutrinos –the building blocks of the universe. Science will eventually prove this as an irrefutable fact. But it will be many years before that happens.

* * *

Imaginary: The power of forming a mental image of something not wholly perceived.

* * *

Thots shape reality.

* * *

Our soul is only complete when both the physical and spiritual aspects of the soul are united. We can go thru life without the guidance of our higher self and many people live that way. But we can become one with our spiritual self, we don't have to wait until death to do so.

* * *

As you go about your daily business, try to touch the Light as often as you can. Keep paper and pen handy and write down ideas as they come to you. Don't trust your memory to keep track of everything. Don't be upset if you don't get ideas right away. Practice makes perfect.

* * *

It's a good idea to have a "Things to Do" list. Organize your time and try to do things in one trip instead of two.

* * *

Do you have a hobby or a pass-time besides watching television? A lot of people look to sports, exercise or Yoga for a diversion. How about doing something creative? There are lots of things you can do that could result in a part-time income. At the least you might make enough to pay for tools and materials. A lot of people have turned a profitable hobby into a thriving business. Just remember the sky's the limit. The broader your horizons the greater your potential will be.

* * *

The more I give the more I get! There have been several times when I lost everything. I always got back more than I lost.

* * *

I don't believe in existing just for the sake of existing. Life has too many possibilities to do absolutely nothing.

* * *

Spirit is primary over the material. We all have our own concept of God. Because, God has many faces. Belief is what's important. Not the type or nature of our belief. Is there one reality or many? Perhaps we won't know until we die. I choose to share my ideas but not to force them on anybody. I hope that you will do the same.

* * *

Mind/Spirit constitutes basic reality. Material things emerge from Mind/Spirit which constitutes true reality. If ideas exist in the Mind. Then objects and situations exist because of consciousness. To be is to be perceived.

Mind/Spirit equals creative ego. It is the ultimate source of reality. It generates change and all knowledge. Absolute Spirit/Reason manifests thru total consciousness in all aspects of existence. Ordinary experience is contradictory. Sometimes reality can only be known thru unique and perhaps mystical experiences. This is called Idealism.

* * *

What it all comes down to is the quality of our thots creates the character of our reality. Thus, we either become prisoners of our own design; or we become eagles soaring above the mean creating our own consequences and potentials.

* * *

Absolutely everything in our experience is the result of thot. Either in the mind of man or the mind of God. The chair you're sitting in, the roof over your head the clothes and shoes you're wearing the car you drive to work and the streets you drive on are all ideas/thots that took form in the mind of some intelligent person. The food you ate for breakfast, the air you breathe, the birds you hear singing, the people you work with all became a reality in the mind of God.

And so, it all comes down to one undeniable fact. Everything in our experience is made up of one thing. That one thing is God/the Light.

In the true reality: we are either one with God or we are all Gods or both.

* * *

Are you one of those people who's going to write a book —sooner or later. If you can find the time to quit staring at the dots on your television set? Are you putting off writing your memoirs Until you've done something interesting?

Guess what? You don't have to have an exciting life to write about your particular slice of life; the interesting people you've met; the mistakes you've made and the lessons you've learned from them; your hopes and dreams and aspirations and the steps you might take to accomplish your goals; and the times you've actually accomplished your objectives.

* * *

We must respect the individual's right to believe as he/she wishes.

* * *

I'm here (exist) because I think I'm here.

* * *

Mind is what connects the spiritual with the material.

* * *

Belief/knowing is the key to everything.

* * *

When setting goals, it is important to determine what is feasible and what is fantasy.

* * *

Today is the tomorrow you worried about yesterday.

* * *

Failure is driven by a sense of unworthiness and fear. Success is inspired by faith and a feeling of oneness with the creator. Mediocrity is motivated by conformity.

* * *

The physical aspect of the soul resides in the brain as mind. It diffuses itself thru out The body to give nourishment. It emanates out of the body and manifests as colored lights. This is your aura.

* * *

When you die, there is a measurable decrease in weight. Albeit nominal, but detectable all the same. Could this decrease in weight account for the soul? How could something spiritual have any weight?

* * *

Mind and emotion are important aspects of our soul. Which is another word for describing the spiritual aspect of our being. It is important to stay in constant contact with our higher self; to increase our personal effectiveness and the exaltation of our complete being. We must strive for a better awareness of our individuality; which is an aspect of universal mind. Not singular but one of the multitudes.

* * *

Who are we really? Do we lose our personality when we become part of the whole or do we gain something? I like to think our individuality is enhanced; when we communicate with others on both the earthly and spiritual planes.

* * *

Good/God created evil to give itself definition. Too many people give the concept of evil the potential to dominate or eliminate the Good; which is never going to happen. It's simply False Evidence Appearing Real—FEAR—evils greatest and most powerful tool.

* * *

Judge others as individuals—don't generalize. Often our first impression of others is correct. However, it is a good idea to reserve judgement and give them a chance to prove us wrong. By no means should we put our guard down. Never trust anybody completely Even our soul mates can be dopple-ganged.

* * *

Never accuse a thinking person of being idle.

* * *

When you perceive a person to be suffering, for any reason. Remember but for the grace of God/the Light, that person could be you. Remember that God never sleeps and hears your every prayer. Bless that person and know that God/the Light will lighten the cross that person must bear, whether it be a pat on the back, a candy bar, a piece of cake, or a few happy tears, that person is going to get something extra because you took the time to bless him/her.

* * *

It's alright to cry—tears cleanse the soul. I have wanted to cry many times when I was happy. But I have never cried because I was unhappy because I have never been truly unhappy. I have wanted to cry when I perceived human suffering, but thus far I've been unable to.

* * *

Too often people blame their mistakes and short-comings on the devil. Using him as an unreal scapegoat. We must take credit for our wrong doing, or we won't be able to recover. It takes a man to admit he's made a mistake.

* * *

We all have our personal demons—we create most of them.

* * *

A lot of people aren't happy unless they want something.

* * *

Open your mind to all possibilities. Refuse to allow negative thots to enter your mind.

* * *

There is always more than one way to do something.

* * *

We have the ability to create miracles in our lives. If we open our minds to the potentials and possibilities. If you're not receptive to the realm of possibilities—you'll fall short of creating miracles; you could otherwise achieve.

* * *

If you believe that you can't do a certain thing; you'll respond to that premise and fail in your efforts. If, on the other hand, you believe that you can—you will eventually succeed in your actions.

* * *

You cannot possess another person.

* * *

Rely upon your inner-self to guide you—in your efforts to achieve your goals.

* * *

An innerknowing guarantees that the thing or situation you seek, will come to fruition at the right time.

* * *

There is an order to the universe. It works in harmony—with or without you. Detach yourself from worldly things; and they will come to you. They will come more easily, with little or no effort on your part.

* * *

Listen to your higher-self; telling you what you should be doing and then make it manifest.

* * *

You have a mission in life. Are you fulfilling it? Or are you just another cog in the wheel of life? Don't just try to fit in with what others think you should be doing. Be true to yourself and be somebody!

* * *

There is no such thing as failure. You simply discovered the wrong way or approach to the given task at hand.

* * *

Fear and love cannot abide together.

* * *

Be true to yourself and be enthusiastic about it. Learn to love yourself and embrace the God within.

* * *

Your thots create your reality. Your thots dictate how you will react to the incidents of your daily life.

* * *

Hate, fear and anger vibrate at lower frequencies. If you are radiating these lower vibrations, you'll get similar feedback from others. Touch the light and emanate the higher frequencies of love and happiness; and you'll get more of the same. This is true because of the law of attraction. As you begin to fill yourself with these happy emotions; you'll find that things become easier for you. Put out happy positive thots to the universe, and it will return like vibrations. The more you give the more you get.

* * *

Each of us has his/her own definition for who/what God is. We must respect the individual's right to believe as he/she wishes. To me God is the Light and the Light is love. So, when you close your eyes and look up and see the bright Light of your soul—know that it mirrors God. You can direct this Light to others. Thus, you can love everybody including your enemies—rendering them harmless.

* * *

Meditating not only has a positive effect on you, but also on those around you as well. Meditating can make you feel more deeply connected to God. You can get off by yourself and commune with nature. There is no better place to meditate than a secluded place among the trees, by a babbling brook, sitting on the grass and looking at the flowers. Meditating brings out your inner peace.

* * *

Remember to live in the now—not the past or the future.

* * *

Problems are often-times a matter of perception. Remember that for every problem there is an answer and an opportunity. Turn your problems over to your higher self for resolution. How do you do that? By meditating. Thru meditation you can attain a state of cosmic consciousness and get a feeling of oneness with all creation. Your feeling of separateness will disappear, and your daily tasks will become easier.

* * *

Any time you allow yourself to be hurt or emotionally upset by other people. You are allowing them to control your feelings. Learn to shield yourself with the Light. And tell them: "No thanks. I don't need your opinion.".

* * *

Don't be offended by what others say to you. They're the ones who have a problem—not you. So, don't embrace it.

* * *

Treat others the way you like to be treated, and they'll treat you the same way.

* * *

Never doubt the power of visualization. The more you focus on your intention; the sooner it will become manifest. Add to this the power of the spoken word and say: "I will have _____"(make your specific request). Put the bright Light of love on your request and remember to tell God "thank you".

* * *

Higher frequencies dissolve lower unwanted frequencies. Happiness resonates at a higher frequency—So be happy!

* * *

The fore-bearer of every action is a thot. So, think in positive terms.

* * *

You create your own reality.

* * *

We would all feel better if we would just think thots that are better.

* * *

You are not alone. You're connected to the source of the universe.

* * *

Before we incarnate we are one with God. We see the life that lies before us and all its potentialities. And, we choose to embrace it. We did this in concert with God.

* * *

We share the same life force with everyone. We all come from God/ the Light—we are all connected.

* * *

God's law is abundance and prosperity. God/the Light wants us to have everything we need and doesn't want us to do without anything. In the realm of Spirit there is no such thing as lack.

* * *

Any problem represents an inability to connect with our higher self. Don't seek the advice of others unless you have a mentor. Let your decisions be between you and your creator. Spiritual advice is available to you at all times. All you need to do is raise your vibrations and ask. Our primary relationship should be with God—effected by working with your higher self—the essence of your being. You do this by meditating.

* * *

Our higher self is in constant communion with God/the Light.

* * *

The feeling of desire must be one of intensity and yearning. Then our higher self will bring what we ask into physical manifestation. We will begin to act upon our vision and receive divine guidance. Our ability to hold on to our inner-vision despite the circumstancses around us will see us thru.

We all have a calling. Do we become actualized or do we ignore the call? Do we follow a course set by others or do we follow the path that take us to our destination? Be eager to listen to your higher self and act on the inspiration. Be grateful for the guidance.

* * *

Inspiration can come from completing tasks and reaching your goals. It also comes from living in the now. Live in the present moment and enjoy the experience. Stay in the now and watch what happens.

* * *

When you want to do something—give it a try. Even if you lose, it's worth the effort. Or, would you rather die wondering what might have happened?

* * *

Spending time doing positive affirmations during meditation is what we need to do in moments of despair. Let go and let God. We also need to pray when times are good. Always remember to tell the Light "Thank You.".

* * *

Live happily in the Light. Bring your dreams into the present moment and begin acting on them. Remember to stairstep your goals and don't bite off more than you can chew.

* * *

Your desire for inspiration stimulates your higher self into action. Because, you've raised the level of your vibrations.

* * *

We are the essence of God/the Light with all that power available to us. If you have an interest in something, go ahead and do it. Your interest is an indication that you have a latent ability to do it and do it well.

* * *

Your excitement and enthusiasm have a direct effect on your vibrations, and your ability to do things. It will bring your hidden talents to the surface.

* * *

Everything we've done or haven't done is in the past. We can either forgive ourselves or carry a sense of unworthiness with us. Many of our spiritual advances come from making mistakes and learning from them.

* * *

Forgiving yourself is essential, if you're going to get to a higher level; and begin to create the things and situations you desire. Think about the people you've wronged. Touch the Light and say: "God bless _____ and let him/her have a wonderful life and many blessings." I believe it helps.

* * *

We are all individualized expressions of God/the Light. We are not the same, but we are still connected. We are unique unto ourselves—bur still connected.

* * *

Begin every day with an expression of gratitude.

* * *

When you pray, you're talking to somebody who cares about what you have to say.

When you're at peace with yourself and the universe you send out vibrations that impact on all living things—even plants!

* * *

Don't be afraid to tell the truth. Most people appreciate honesty.

* * *

Be selective in your television viewing. Do you really need to hear all the bad things they tell you on the evening news? Do you really need to be exposed to all the violence that pervades television programming? Watch the comedy programs—laughter is the best medicine! And, check out the programs on PBS.

* * *

Giving and receiving go hand in hand. They revolve in a continuous cycle.

* * *

Taking action is the best way to improve our connection to our higher self. The key to being in Spirit is movement.

* * *

Don't quit—don't give up on yourself. Get your blood circulating and do the things you've been putting off. Don't give in to fear—don't let it stop you. Never give up!

* * *

God is the Light. The Light is love.

* * *

We attract what we focus on. If we concentrate on lack, then we shall have a shortage. If we choose to see an abundant supply, then we shall have opulence.

* * *

God's healing power is within you. All you have to do is ask. This is not to say that you shouldn't go to doctors and take medications for these may be the avenues that God chose to help you.

* * *

Pray without ceasing.

* * *

Approach our creator (the Light) with an open mind and a willingness to follow the advice that comes from our higher self.

* * *

There is no them—there is only us—we are all connected. There is only One.

* * *

With God all things are possible.

* * *

Happiness can be found in setting goals and striving to achieve them. Never be satisfied with status-quo. Make a list of the goals you expect to achieve and set a date for when you expect to achieve them. Write them down and keep them in your pocket. When you attain your goal set a new one—to keep the spice in your life.

* * *

Belief at the beginning of a venture guarantees success. Visualize what you want to do and the stepping stones you will take to get there. Know that you have what it takes to accomplish your goal. Belief is what creates our realities.

* * *

No set back can hold a positive thinking person back for long. The harder they fall the greater they bounce back. It is their belief in themselves and God/the Light that makes the difference. These people do not allow negative thots to dissuade them.

* * *

Positive thinkers are alive with the zest for life. They know that with the help of God/the Light they can overcome any obstacle.

* * *

When you are confronted with a problem, confront it with the confidence that you have the ability to resolve it successfully. The positive thinker has the right mindedness to overcome even the most stressful problem.

* * *

Problems must be attacked repeatedly with a positive attitude and faith that God/the Light is helping you. Never give up!

There is a mutual law of attraction. Like attracts like. There-fore negative thots will attract negative things. And positive thots will attract positive things. This is simple cause and effect.

* * *

Positive thinking is the mental and spiritual means by which the individual can move from apparent failure to success and accomplishment.

* * *

Achievers always have a goal. They work towards that goal in a relentless way; and won't take no for an answer. They have enthusiasm for what they're doing. They never give up. They are believers and never doubt what they are doing. They don't think negative things. They are achievers and get results.

* * *

Achievement is obtained thru an intense and burning desire to succeed. Backed by faith in a God, who helps those who help themselves. Be a positive thinker who sets goals and reaches them.

* * *

To reach your goals, you must have a strong belief that it can be done.

* * *

You can never accomplish more than you can dream. So then dream big and then act on those dreams. Believe in yourself and your ability to accomplish big things.

* * *

Attitude is extremely important. It reflects how you think and believe. Before you can do anything, you must make a mental and spiritual commitment to your goal. You need to maintain a positive attitude on the way to attaining your goals. Affirm your intention to reaching your goals. Imagine yourself succeeding with God's help. Dispel all negative thots. Don't allow difficulties to have any power over you. Believe in yourself.

* * *

I can do all things thru God—who strengthens me.

* * *

External manifestations match internal thot vibrations.

* * *

Give what you can, and God's abundance will come to you.

When things are not going well, it is because we are out of contact with the creative forces. All we must do is establish a better contact with God's endless supply of abundance. Raise your level of vibration. Ask your higher self to help you by giving you inspiration.

* * *

Banish all anxiety from your mind, by repeating positive affirmations and getting back to nature. Take your family for a Sunday drive and buy everybody an ice cream cone.

* * *

Never think or say anything negative. Dwelling on negative thots— even for a moment can ward off the good things in life. Occupy your thots with bright, happy and positive things. Open your mind to the good that God will supply you with. Be a creative thinker. Never think of anything that you don't want to manifest in your life.

* * *

Your subconscious mind will strive to serve you with what you're thinking about. Discipline your thinking to attract only desirable things and situations. Your success is contingent upon the quality of your thots.

* * *

Nothing is impossible for the believer. We are greater than anything that can befall us.

* * *

We have the power to overcome any situation and make things better. Remember you are a winner in the game of life.

* * *

You can excel and become bigger than your failures and disappointments. Remember there is a lesson to be found in everything. You have the power to turn present circumstances in your favor.

* * *

You cannot change a situation until you change yourself… be positive!

* * *

Today is your day—make it count for something!

* * *

Enthusiasm and gratitude are two of the greatest attributes we can have.

* * *

Life is not really about what happens to you, but what you do about what happens to you.

* * *

You have latent creative powers lying dormant within you. Take them out, dust them off and use them! Don't deny your potential. Take a positive outlook and go for it! Seize the day.

* * *

Don't bury your talents under a ton of negative thinking. Be positive and you will see the opportunities available to you. Make the most of every day and all situations.

* * *

We all have the power deep within us to make a difference in other people's lives. Always expect the best.

* * *

Today may contain the biggest opportunity of your life. The decisions you make today will affect your future.

* * *

You can get fantastic results if you believe that today is your day. Take advantage of the opportunities that come your way.

* * *

You are only human. You are going to have your down sides—it's only natural. Don't give into them; or put up with them. Stimulate your thinking with positive thots, and mentally tell the negative feelings to go away. It's that simple! You'll soon learn which techniques work best for you. You must really want to overpower the disheartening thots; because there can be an odd comfort in thinking limited thots. It is easy to quit trying, but it is just as easy to keep working towards your goals. Don't escape reality and bask in self-pity. Don't wallow in your depressed thots. Call on your higher self to help you climb out of the dismal gloom you find yourself in.

* * *

Thirty-five years ago I had a goal: to go one minute without having a negative thot. (I was that bad off!) it took several weeks to accomplish that goal. My next goal was to go five minutes without a negative thot; Then after that ten minutes etc. I am pleased to say I never have any negative thots at all. And I'm here to tell you—it's a great feeling!

* * *

When despair overwhelms you and threatens to take over your life. Find some kind person to talk to. Someone who will listen to you pour your heart out. It may be a friend or a lover, a psychiatrist or a minister. But find someone to talk to. If you can't find someone to talk to... talk to God. God always listens and is available twenty-four hours a day.

* * *

The way out of any debilitating situation is to face it head on and take corrective action. It is not the situation that is important—it's about how you think about and react to the situation that counts. When you begin to think in a positive fashion—you can take steps to resolve the problem.

* * *

Look for advantages in what seems to be a hopeless situation and act on them. You can pray your way out of any dismal circumstance. Remember that God/ the Light allows us to have problems, so we can learn from them.

* * *

Positive thinking is a crucial process that is guaranteed to keep your spirits lofty and unstoppable. Be creative, no matter what circumstances you find yourself in. You should never be overcome by problems; for each one carries a solution and an opportunity. Hence a Problem is not something to run from; but a simple matter to be addressed and taken advantage of. Turn your problems into assets. There is an answer for every problem. Just persevere until you solve the riddle.

* * *

If your scraping the bottom of the barrel—rejoice for the only way that lies before you is up! Hardship is a great tutor—it can teach you valuable lessons.

* * *

Never construct an argument against yourself. Learn to love yourself and everyone around you—because we're all part of God/the Light.

* * *

Positive thinkers acquire the ability to think rationally and see things thru.

* * *

Positive thinkers get to feeling down sometimes, but they have attained the ability to keep their thinking functional instead of dysfunctional. By merit of a sound mind, they can forget the bad things and deal with the business at hand.

* * *

You can achieve success after failure. All you have to do is regroup and think about what you did right and try, try again.

* * *

If you have the right attitudes and beliefs, you can achieve success. After what seems like failure don't say: "if only" say: "Next time I'll do it the right way.".

* * *

Be a believer in miracles—there is no such thing as impossible. Think in terms of "I can". nothing is too good to be true.

* * *

Often what seems to be negative and destructive turns out to be an asset. And, that asset wouldn't have manifest, if something hadn't happened that seemed like a detriment at first.

* * *

If you have faith as a mustard seed… nothing will be impossible for you.

* * *

Drop the idea of impossible focus on the possible.

* * *

We are what we think and what we think will become manifest. Positive thinking creates the best in terms of possibilities.

* * *

Learn to read the thots that are most prevalent in your mind. In time the creative currents will make them manifest. Remember like attracts like. What you think creates your future. Thots manifest into actualization. Your thots are invisible, but if you wait long enough you can see them come into being.

* * *

In creating your desire, first you must want the thing or situation with a great intensity –be specific about what you want. Set a date for its materialization. Visualize the thing or situation as already having come into being and act accordingly.

* * *

Petition God/the Light to help you in all your endeavors. Say "I cannot effect these changes on my own. I need your help.".

* * *

If we can adopt bad ideas from negative programing. We can also get rid of them, by countering each bad idea with: "That's not true—be gone and don't come back! You have no power over me." Substitute a positive affirmation to replace the negative thot. It may take many times to refute the negative programing—but, it's worth the effort. Don't you think?

* * *

Positive thinkers love life and create wonderful things to fill up their days. You can too!

* * *

An invisible power links the physical, mental and spiritual realms. Recognizing this power affects your health and welfare.

* * *

God wants us to be well and healthy and have the best that life has to offer. Acquiring good health can be a spiritual endeavor. A healthy spirit is conducive to providing a healthy mind and body.

Negative emotions and attitudes can make you unhealthy, both mentally and physically. You can use positive thinking to ward off illness and keep negative forces at bay. Choosing to do this requires clear and disciplined thinking.

* * *

Our physical health is determined greatly by what we think.

* * *

Your physical, mental and spiritual well-being can be affected by God's healing power.

* * *

Gaining a positive attitude and maintaining it is prompted by an intense desire to do so.

* * *

To the creative thinker, there is always a way.

* * *

It is hard to imagine overcoming negative thinking without relying on faith and prayer. God/ the Light stands ready to help anyone who asks.

* * *

In everything you do give yourself up to it.

* * *

Happiness is attained by acquiring a calm mental outlook. Know that you can handle anything that come up.

* * *

Fear, worry and anxiety can immobilize you and put you in the gutter. You must have confidence in yourself. Know that with God's help you can overcome any obstacle.

* * *

The world in which we live was created by our thot patterns. If we seek a happy and joyful life, we must entertain thots that produce happiness and joy.

* * *

Do you have a dream? How long have you had it? Have you acted on it? Maybe it's time you did. Dreams are the stuff that reality is made of.

* * *

Look around you… virtually everything you use on a daily basis began as a dream: electricity indoor plumbing, light bulbs, your car etc. Need I go on? Dreams are the fore-bearers of possibilities made reality.

* * *

When you're goal setting, determine which dreams are feasible and which are fantasies. Then decide which ones are immediate and which are long term goals. Be open minded about the time and effort necessary to attain these goals. Layout the stepping stones needed to reach your destination. Then take one step at a time. Do everything to the best of your ability.

* * *

Choose goals that will benefit others besides yourself.

* * *

Nothing is going to happen until you make it happen. No matter how difficult your goals are—you can do it! By taking the first step, you can overcome that old enemy—fear. There is nothing to fear but fear itself.

* * *

Don't get discouraged when striving for your goal. Outline the steps you must take and then take them one at a time—no matter how bad you want to quit—keep going. Persistence is important because not much of importance is accomplished without it.

* * *

The difference between success and failure can be the willingness to go the extra mile.

* * *

If we broadcast positive thots—by the law of attraction, positive things will come to us. Positive vibrations beget positive feedback. The time to do it is now. The quality of your thots will create a new world around you.

* * *

Before you go to sleep at night, see yourself as a winner in the game of life—doing the things you want to do, and helping others to do the same. We tend to become the person we imagine ourselves to be. Always be a positive thinker—it will put you where you want to be.

* * *

You can recreate your self-image by thinking of yourself as exceptionally competent. Visualization is the key to everything.

* * *

When you think of yourself as a good person deserving the best of everything; others will subconsciously pick up on your high self-esteem and treat you accordingly.

* * *

Peace of mind is important to everybody. How do you get it? By focusing on God. Anxiety cannot exist when your mind revolves around the Light. This is the condition you must create in order for your inner peace to grow.

* * *

Your attitude toward the conditions that surround you is more important than the conditions themselves. When you respond to a given circumstance in a negative manner the situation can and will get worse. Peace of mind, on the other hand, will help to wash the problem away. Call upon the calmness of God/the Light to get rid of the tension that has built up inside you.

* * *

Keep in mind that God/the Light loves and cares about us. God will impel you to great heights, if you call on that spiritual power for help. If you contemplate God's power and ability to help you—it will happen.

* * *

Positive anticipation is closely aligned to the higher self and can affect all possibilities in a positive way. What you think will become manifest.

* * *

Positive thinkers don't look backwards. They think about tomorrow and what the can do today to facilitate it.

* * *

Be a person who genuinely cares about other people; and other people will begin to care about you.

* * *

Ari

The greatest challenge in life is life itself. The problems of life either makes us larger or smaller. Some people fold under pressure others set examples. Do you have the power to face up to the trials that life has to offer? Of- course you do!

* * *

Face up to your problems—don't hide from them. Problems don't go away, they get worse. Meet your problems head on. Take them apart and analyze them. Find their weakness and defeat them. With help from God/ the Light…. You can do so.

* * *

Take a good look inward. Are you carrying a load of guilt around with you? You may have to go to a counselor or a minister to unload your guilt. There is a benefit that comes with confession. It gives you the opportunity to get forgiveness from God/the Light.

* * *

Act upon your convictions and chase fear away. Banish fear from your life by using positive affirmations backed by positive action.

* * *

The power within is the greatest power in the universe… it is transmitted by positive affirmations (prayer). The power that comes to us thru prayer is available to all of us. Negative thinking and amoral behavior can block it from coming. So, can self-centeredness. Become a person who seeks to help others.

* * *

Envelope everything you do with prayer. That is the true key to happiness.

* * *

Enthusiasm is very important. You should carry it over to everything you do. Enthusiasm activates the power within you. If you find it hard to be enthusiastic, you may be wondering how to get that way. Just act as tho you have it and sooner or later it will come naturally to you. Enthusiasm makes a big difference in everything you think, say and do. It will press you forward to achievement in your self-elected tasks and goals.

* * *

What your mind can conceive –you can achieve!

* * *

If you keep your enthusiasm up—you'll never think about giving up. Be enthusiastic about everything. Intensity of desire is essential to tapping the power within. Top achievers—the winners of this world give their best in everything they do. They never quit trying. They just keep on keeping it up—they never give up.

* * *

How do you get to feeling happy? By developing a child-like attitude towards life. Children have a sense of wonder that brings happiness.

* * *

How does a winner become a winner? By trying and keeping on trying until they get the desired results. They never give up—they are persistent. They try to do their best. They never compete with the other guy—they compete with themselves. They try to do better today than yesterday.

* * *

Motivation makes top achievers what they are. It helps you overcome difficulties and the pitfalls that life has to offer. Motivation gives you the belief that you can accomplish the task at hand –no matter what the obstacles are.

* * *

How do you stay healthy? For one thing, stay busy. Second, eat right. Walking and exercise are also essential. An intense spiritual awareness is crucial. A life free from worry is very valuable when it comes to health. Guilt and anger can affect your health adversely You have to purge these negative emotions from your mind.

`* * *

Thru positive visualization, we can attain perfect health in both body and mind. Your inner power—your spiritual self will strive to provide the results you ask for.

* * *

You can turn set-backs into something positive; you have the inner power to do so. God/the Light will make you greater than you thot was possible. Always believe that God/the Light is helping you. Know that you have the power to do what must be done. Visualize yourself as having the power to do so. You are greater than your problems. Your problems contain hidden opportunities.

* * *

Always seek to help others; and, they will be there when you need help.

* * *

Never give on living. Your inner power will give up on you if you do. Keep in touch with the wonderful world around you. Embrace new ideas and try different ways to be creative. Take the time to help other people. Live each day one at a time. Begin to look for the opportunity that each day holds.

* * *

Miracles come those who program their mind with positive affirmations.

* * *

Develop the God given power within and you will have a magnificent and creative life.

* * *

Break your objective up into little goals and accomplish these little goals one after another. Eventually they'll add up to the big objective.

* * *

Develop the God given power within and you can have a magnificent and creative life.

* * *

Want to change your personality? First decide what traits you want to possess. Hold that image of yourself having those qualities; hold it firmly in your mind. Then begin acting as tho you have those traits. Finally, believe that you have those characteristics. Ask for help and thank the Light for assisting you. Act on the premise of what you imagine yourself to be and hold it firmly in your mind. You will over a period, become the person you want to be. Assuming you remain faithful to the process.

* * *

All you have to do is think and act as tho you have enthusiasm and sooner or later you will have it.

* * *

A goal with a purpose is the best inspiration a person can have.

* * *

Cultivate a love of life and love God. Fill your life with meaning—for life is good.

* * *

Proper self-image provides a good positive alternative to self-doubt and feelings of inadequacy. You must sell yourself on yourself and be enthusiastic about it. Come to the realization of your own worth.

* * *

Believe that you will reach your goal. Visualize it as already happening and it will happen. Love your job and the people associated with it. Who knows? You may get a promotion!

* * *

Enthusiasm for the possibilities that exist in life increases your potential. Become excited about the opportunities your job has to offer and open new horizons.

* * *

Belief is the key to the successful, undertaking of any goal. Remember to thank the Light for helping.

* * *

A good mental attitude in the face of adversity is of primary importance in solving the problems life has to offer. Attitude is more important than facts. Look for the power within to solve your problems.

* * *

Let go and let God.

* * *

Persistence is the answer to successful living. No matter what happens—don't give up! Get your competitive spirit flowing. Always look to move forward in your efforts to do the task at hand. Never settle for less than what you want.

* * *

Suffering can make you strong and mature. But why should we suffer when we have the power of the Light to guide us? Be enthusiastic about your potential to overcome problems and emerge the victor. Thru positive thinking and right living we can become the superstars we were meant to be.

* * *

Nobody gets something for nothing. Be prepared to offer goods or service for what you want.

* * *

It's not whether you experience defeat but in how you handle it. You can turn defeat into something positive; from which you can gain a better more intelligent approach to life. Amazing things happen to those who think constructively.

* * *

The kingdom of God is within you.

* * *

You are bigger than the problems that face you. Believe and have faith that God/the Light is within you at all times and wants the best for you and will help you get it. We all have the potential to solve problems. Negative attitudes and emotions can block that God given power. So, it necessary to dispel negative thots and replace them with positive affirmations such as: "God is within me and has the power to diminish all my problems.". Visualize yourself as having or doing that which you desire.

* * *

If you have financial problems—don't freak out. Know that God/the Light is with you and will help you overcome the problem. Work out a budget and make arrangements for a payment plan. Cut out all frivolous spending.

* * *

Don't visualize negative things happening. Instead, picture good things coming to pass. Take each negative thot and tear it apart. Look for the opportunity it contains and then dismiss it. Forget and release the negative idea; each time it comes back repeat the process. Eventually It won't come back. Remember to substitute something positive to take its place.

* * *

Conceiving an objective is the first step towards attaining success. The second is planning and preparing. The third step is taking action. The final step is knowing/believing that you will reach your goal. Set a date for which you expect to accomplish your objective. Visualize, visualize, visualize…

* * *

People who want to get ahead need a strong self-image to support them in their quest. But they also need to convey that impression to others, especially to those they work with and for. See yourself as a success… There's no better way to be!

* * *

Whatever you desire—pray for it. And when you pray believe that you shall receive it and you shall have it. Always remember to give thanks for what you ask.

* * *

Forgiveness is an important factor in anything we do. Sometimes it is hard to forgive someone who has wronged us—but it is critical to do so, because the resentment that your carry can create blocks. The way I do it is to see the light and then direct it to that person. Remember the Light is love. Eventually you will find the anger and resentment to be fading and sooner or later will be nonexistent. So there you have it—a simple easy way to forgive others.

* * *

More importantly we need to learn to forgive ourselves, for our wrong doing. Touch the Light and say I forgive myself or what I did to _____. Then send that person the Light and say: "May that person have a wonderful life and many blessings.". Do this as often as you think about it and eventually the bad memory will fade away.

* * *

There is an epidemic that faces this nation it is called "tension". Here is an exercise that can help you relieve tension—you can do it sitting or laying down. Begin with your toes and feet. Talk to your body and say: "my toes are relaxed". Then move up thru your body talking to it as you go along first tense the muscles and then relax them telling them as you go along to relax. Tense and relax your feet, your ankles, your calves, your knees, thighs, groin stomach, your torso your biceps forearms hands and fingers. Finally tense and relax your shoulders, neck and face your ears and eyes. Then relax completely and feel a gentle breeze blowing over your body. Hear the birds singing and visualize a lake—calm and peaceful, the waves gently lapping at the shore. Imagine the trout jumping at the mosquitos. Be still and know that God/the Light is with you, cares about you and will take care of you.

* * *

Pray without ceasing—visualize thru-out the day.

* * *

Visualize yourself as someone who is command of your life. You'll increase your chances of being that kind of person—as you should be.

* * *

God/the Light gave us a magnificent computer for a mind. It has been programed to do anything we desire. The problem is: we get negative input from others that disrupts the original program and keeps it from working properly. What we must do is hit the delete button, when anything negative comes up. Replace the negative thot with something positive and repeat it three or four times. Eventually your mind will begin working properly— the way it's supposed to.

* * *

Shake off the old limiting labels that people have placed on you. Be the person that God/the Light made you to be—a winner—a leader—a somebody! Be that somebody and step out from the sea of mediocrity and excel like you were intended to do.

* * *

You can be transformed from what you are to what you want to be—what God wants you to be. All you must do is form a picture of the exalted you. Hold it firmly in your mind and tell yourself: "That's who I was meant to be and by God's will that's who I'm becoming.".

* * *

When you wake up say: "Today is the day God has made for me. It's going to be a great day. I'm excited for good things are going to happen to me on this day.".

* * *

Now it's time for you to do something great. God/the Light put something in you that must come to fruition. All you have to do is just let it happen. Take the first step toward your goal, then take the second step. As you progress, you may meet some opposition. Go around the obstacles that try to discourage you. Don't take no for an answer. Sooner or later, you'll reach your destination. Once you have accomplished your task—set another goal and go at it the same way.

* * *

I believe that before we incarnate we are one with God. And, we see the life that lies before us with all its potentialities. And, we agree to embrace it. This is not predestination, for we are blessed with free will and can choose to go on a different path if we want.

* * *

Your dream can become manifest, especially if it includes helping others in the process. If God's law is one of abundance; it doesn't hurt to ask for a little more to give to charity. Remember that there are people out here that are not as well off as you are and could use a little help.

* * *

What you have right now is all you need to fulfill your destiny. If you need more next week, God/the Light will see that you get it. Take appraisal of what you have and you will see that you have what you need to get thru today. Stairstep your goals and you will see that you get what you need from moment to moment. So, don't hesitate to take the first step into your future.

* * *

Don't let misfortune or discouragement get you down. Remember you are a child of God and deserve the best life has to offer. Now—go out and get it!!!

* * *

Be grateful for the blessings you've received: The time you were down and out and got a helping hand; the time you got a promotion you didn't think you deserved; the time you could have been killed in a traffic accident; the time you met the love of your life; your children. I'm sure you could add many more things to this list. Be grateful and know that many more blessings are coming to you.

* * *

There is an obvious connection between what we think and feel physically. If we think negative and critical thots, we can get emotionally and physically ill. On the other hand, if we think positive and happy thots we can become physically and emotionally exhilarated. Watch God/the light work things out for you.

* * *

Seek and you shall find… knock and the door shall be opened.

* * *

Choosing to live righteously does not mean that it happens with no effort on our part. The efforts we make can be inspired by God/the Light. We are never asked to do anything without being empowered to do so.

* * *

We sometimes allow outside sources to control our thinking. But we can create positive thots to substitute for the limiting thots of others. It actually requires very little effort. However, it does require discipline and persistence.

* * *

Choose to think good happy thots every day. Expel negative and limiting thots, the minute they surface. An idle mind is the devils workshop.

* * *

When striving to do the right thing, we sometimes meet with discouragement. Don't give up. Your diligence puts you one day closer to success.

* * *

A joyful life is contingent upon the thots you choose to think. All aspects of life are connected to your mind.

* * *

Believe and you will receive.

* * *

Don't accept failure, illness or disease. Fight back with positive affirmations and affirmative action. We can overcome all obstacles with help from God/the Light. We can wallow in self-pity or we can petition a higher power for help. Take responsibility and take charge of your life. Sometimes you won't get an answer to your prayers for a long time. Persevere and have faith.

* * *

Difficulty comes to all of us at one time or another. We have no choice but to keep on trying. Sooner or later we'll get it right.

* * *

Don't leave your tasks for the other guy to do. Take pride in your work and give it your best shot. Practice makes perfect. Maintain an "I can" attitude in everything you do. Attitudes really do make a difference.

* * *

God/the Light has made us a promise: never to give us more than we can handle.

* * *

We need to focus on the task at hand and exclude everything else. You can't do two things at the same time and have either of them turn out right. Concentration takes discipline. Sometimes we get our priorities mixed up, and we must recoup and refocus. Make sure you're doing what you really want to do.

* * *

To accomplish an important task, try to be alone if possible. Try to start early. Make a list of things to do after you're finished. Don't answer the phone. Take a break every two hours and do some stretching exercises. Eat a light lunch and drink lots of water. When you're done, you can make yourself available to others and answer your phone messages. But when you're busy it's important to maintain your focus and not give in to distractions.

* * *

If you want to have good friends, be the type of person you would like to be around. Compliment others and listen closely to what they have to say. Avoid contact with negative people and stay away from people who try to bring you down to their level.

* * *

God/the Light knows that you have great potential. Don't dwell on your mistakes—as an individual you are more right than wrong. Take the time to evaluate yourself and you will see that you are an awesome person, deserving the best that life has to offer. The way we think about ourselves affects us in many different ways. God loves you so why wouldn't you love yourself? Don't try to make yourself pay for your mistakes—there is a lesson to be learned from them. So, learn the lesson. Then forget and release the memory.

* * *

God is watching you and sees your every move. God/the Light is willing to help you, if you only ask.

* * *

Our attitudes can make our problems insurmountable or like a "piece of cake. It all depends on whether you take a positive or negative approach to them. We can rise above our present circumstances, if we maintain a positive point of view. On the other hand, if we take a negative approach— we will surely fail.

* * *

Don't take people at face value—get to know them and find out what they're really like. You may wind-up with a valuable friend. We can all benefit by broadening our horizons.

* * *

Each and every one of us is an individual with qualities unique unto ourselves. It would be boring if we were all the same. Compliment others for their personality traits, and remember we are all connected.

* * *

Worry and stress can have a tremendous impact on our health and emotional well-being. Turn to self-help books (or the Bible) for inspiration and direction. What's on your mind and your anxiety level are closely related. Worry can make things worse. Do your positive affirmations, stretching exercises, spend some time in quiet meditation or simply turn on some music and dance your cares away.

* * *

Can happiness really affect your health? I know so, for medical science has proved it many times in their studies. Negative feelings can affect your health adversely. So be happy… it's as simple as that!

* * *

If we give up in our efforts to get ahead, we miss out on the best part of life. So, hang in there and give it your best shot. Don't wait until tomorrow—do it now!

* * *

If you anticipate something you have to do with anxiety. You either won't do it or you'll do it poorly. Dreading doing that thing can make you feel pulverized. Go into a state of meditation and see yourself taking the steps you need to take to accomplish the task. Feel a great sense of satisfaction that comes with a job well done. Ask God/the Light to help you; take a deep breath and do it.

* * *

Thots of fear can get us down and prevent us from doing the best job possible. They can drain our energy and make us depressed. Believe in God/the Light and watch things happen for the best.

* * *

We can raise our level of energy by repeating positive affirmations during our period of meditation. Good thots will definitely help us to get up and get going.

* * *

Each day when we get up, we are given a new opportunity to do what's right and get ahead. The mistakes we made yesterday are behind us and have no power over us. There may be lessons to be learned and those lessons will put us ahead.

* * *

Don't compare yourself to others. You don't have to be like someone else. Just be yourself and be happy with that. Learn to like yourself and you will find it easier to like others.

* * *

Free will is a gift we are given at birth; what we do with it is up to us. We know right from wrong and what to do at any point in time. God/the Light is always watching us and hoping the best for us; but allows us to make mistakes and learn to correct them for ourselves as best we can. However, we can petition God/ the Light for help and that's what we should be doing.

* * *

We must reaffirm our belief each and every day. The best time to do it so is before we get out of bed.

* * *

We can change our lives by making the right choices. God/the Light will always guide you; if you ask for help. As we become reborn into the Light, it becomes easy to recognize destructive thinking and correct it.

* * *

Think before you speak are sound words of advice. Consider the impact your words will have on others. Anticipate what they will say to you in return—if you say a certain thing. It is always good to pay compliments in your conversations.

* * *

When we are engulphed with too many things to do; we may lose our temper and even say things we don't mean or worse yet have a tantrum. Don't give yourself more than you can handle. Do one thing at a time—multi-tasking isn't anything to brag about. Know your limitations and act accordingly.

* * *

Affirmation is a device by which we can let others know that we appreciate who they are and the things they do. Everyone appreciates a compliment.

* * *

When dealing with people, remember you are relating to a creature of emotion. Be careful not to insult or infuriate that person. Who knows what can happen—if you do.

* * *

The strongest craving in human nature is the desire to be appreciated. Why not raise the self-esteem of our loved ones and associates?

* * *

In all your affairs get the other persons point of view and merge it with your own. Remember there is always a third alternative for every situation. Focus on the needs and desires of the other person. Look at things from their perspective. Seek ways where both of you can benefit.

* * *

If you want to win friends—put yourself out to help others.

* * *

Put a smile on your face and you will find that people will return it. Your smile will cheer up everyone who sees it. Do you do some of your work on the telephone? Put a smile in your voice and people will notice it.

* * *

Be a good listener—most people like to talk about themselves; their problems, hopes, dreams, aspirations and experiences. You will earn the reputation of being a good conversationalist. And, who knows—you might learn something.

* * *

Make people feel important and show a genuine interest in them. Encourage them to talk about themselves. Inquire about their interests and make them feel valuable.

* * *

Allow the other person to be right—even if they're wrong. What would you rather have… a shallow victory or a friend? Change the subject—talk about things you can both agree upon take the time to think the situation thru and consider the others point of view. Who knows? They may be right. Is there merit in their opinion?

* * *

The desire to excel is in all of us. We all want praise and recognition. You can inspire others by pointing out what they do well and by telling them you have confidence in them. Give them a reputation to live up to. Be generous with your compliments. Always make people happy about doing what you ask.

* * *

We all limit our potential living below our capabilities. We are unique and have latent abilities; that would allow us to soar far above mediocrity. Each of us is an individual—truly one of a kind.

* * *

Learn to prioritize and do the important things first. Delegate authority to those who can help you. Worry, tension and anxiety can break you down and make you feel exhausted. Don't try to do more than you can handle. Take time out to relax. Relax your entire body from head to toe—especially the eyes. How do you do that? Just lean back and get comfortable. Close your eyes and let go. Talk to each part of your body and tell it to relax. Take about ten minutes to do it. You will notice the difference in how you feel.

* * *

Act as if your happy when doing boring, mundane jobs. The more you act the happier you'll feel. Congratulations! You've just formed a positive, new habit. Approach your work with enthusiasm and you'll be surprised at what you can accomplish.

* * *

Celebrate your oneness with God/the Light and the universe. Remember we're all connected. What we think, say and do has a profound effect on others.

* * *

Never stop being yourself—don't try to be somebody else. Find out who you truly are and implement the personality traits that will put you on top. Ask yourself: "what are the aspects of my personality that will help me excel in my chosen undertaking? How can I make them work for me?".

* * *

Effective communication is essential in any and every situation. Go directly to the person involved and avoid using the grapevine to get your ideas across. Be receptive to other peoples' ideas and thank them for contributing. It sometimes takes work to keep an open line of communication—but it's worth it. The skilled communicator always listens to what the other person has to say.

* * *

The competent communicator finds out what the other person wants and shows them how to get it. The most important thing people want is admiration and respect and to be regarded as a person of importance. You can help that person excel in what they're doing if you give them motivation and tell them how great they are. Tell them they're doing an awesome job. Seek their opinions and delegate the power to make decisions. Show them you respect their abilities; by giving them some elbow room. Demonstrate that you have confidence in them by telling them you trust them to make the right choices.

How do you get other people to do what you want? By instilling burning desire to please you. Give them credit for what they do. People need to be recognized for what they accomplish. Get them to be interested in what they're doing and take it from there.

We all have a little child within us that craves appreciation. Give them what they need: a compliment, a pat on the back and some encouragement.

Praise doesn't cost anything, but it's worth more than gold to the person that gets it.

* * *

Express an interest in other people and they'll become interested in you. Be sincere in your concern—it will pay off in the long run.

* * *

Look at the total picture from the other person's perspective. What experience does that person have? What do they hope to accomplish? What are they searching for? Seek to help them overcome their problems. People respond to those who listen to them. Listening is tremendously important. It's a skill you need to cultivate. Communication begins with listening.

* * *

People need to feel what they contribute is of vital importance. They need to get recognition for it. Treat people with respect and you'll get the best from them. Remember we're all human.

* * *

Winners set goals and reach them. How do they do that??? They visualize what they want to accomplish. Then they layout the stepping stones that will take them where they want to go. They continue to visualize, visualize, visualize. Do this as often as you can as you stairstep your efforts. Don't take no for an answer. If you run into obstacles—go around them. Never give up. When you reach your goal—set another one and go at it the same way. If you stand still—you'll get old and won't be able to enjoy the life you created. Your goals should be down to earth and doable.

* * *

Keep your life in balance at all times. Make time for family friends and relaxation. Don't give all your time to work. If you want to excel in business. You must focus on all aspects of your life—not just work. Pretty soon your kids will grow up and won't have time for you—if you don't take time for them now. Your spouse will drift away if you don't go out on Saturday nights. When it comes to time out for your family—there are no excuses! Say to yourself: "the most important things in life are myself and my family." and say it often. Leisure time and family should be top priority. Make an effort to spend as much time planning your time off as you do for your work. Doing so will make you happier.

* * *

External circumstances do not determine what will become of us. It's how we react to them that makes the difference.

* * *

People want to be associated with self-achievers. They're attracted to confident, happy, positive people. The powerful attitude of an achiever is contagious, and it rubs off on others. A positive attitude can be transferred from one person to another. Pretty soon it catches fire, and everyone gets involved.

* * *

A positive attitude is important in every aspect of your life. Don't let a negative attitude occupy your mind. Say to the thot: "You're not welcome here—you're not invited. I release you –don't come back!". Place a positive thot to replace the negative one, you just displaced.

* * *

Worry which can cause anxiety and depression is one of the biggest problems that faces us today. Many people are worried about losing their house, their job or their car. What can be done about it? Come up with a contingency plan; something you can fall back on. Put a portion of your income into a savings account—as a buffer, in case you need it. Cut out all frivolous spending. You might want to consolidate your bills. Develop a worse- case scenario and know what you're going to do, if disaster strikes— be prepared for the worst. Then put those plans in the back of your mind.

Smug in the knowledge that you'll make it no matter what happens. Then get back to positive thinking—visualize what you do want… a new car? A promotion? Be generous with yourself and remember that God/the Light wants the best for you. Maintain a picture of what you do want. Think about the stepping stones you will need to accomplish your goals. Then go for it!

* * *

Focus on the needs of others. That's a sure way of getting your mind off your problems and it will help you like yourself better.

* * *

Try to excel in everything you do. Who gets the promotion– the guy who's just getting by or the person who goes the extra mile?

* * *

Enthusiasm is contagious—it can spread like wildfire. There is no better way to get a job done right, than being enthusiastic about it. And, guess what? You'll get compliments for a job well done—there may even be a promotion in the offing.

Enthusiasm comes from within. How do you get enthusiasm? You can act as if you have it. Think of things to like about what you're doing— think about what interests you and focus on being happy. You'll find that enthusiasm will bubble over to all other aspects of your life.

* * *

When you have a problem look at the situation from all angles— get to know it like the back of your hand. Learn the benefits and see the possibilities—broaden your horizons and then give it your best shot. If it doesn't work the first time—try again and use the proverbial "elbow grease". Be excited about what you're doing. Enthusiasm guarantees success in whatever you're doing.

* * *

Happiness takes commitment and discipline. What does happiness mean to you? Freedom from worry... a custom-built home... a new car... finding your soulmate... or perhaps a promotion would make you happy. But maybe, when you've accomplished your objective and the newness has worn off—you're not as elated as you'd thot you'd be. One thing you can do is set another goal. You can find happiness in striving for a new objective. But perhaps you're not happy because of some problem hidden deep within the subconscious mind. Now, it's time for meditation to discover insights as to why you're not happy. Ask your higher self to reveal what is troubling you at the subconscious level. It may be something from your childhood or there's something missing in your relationships. Sooner or later, you'll discover the problem. Take it apart—dissect it—look at it from every perspective. Once you've discovered the problem—decide what to do about it. The solution may be something simple or you may have to seek help from a mental health practitioner or a minister. When you get to the root of the problem you'll be able to solve it. Then forget and release the problem and go happily about your business.

* * *

Remember to stairstep your goals never biting off more than you can handle. Don't forget to visualize—see yourself having or doing what you so desire. Do this as often as your busy schedule will allow. When you have the picture set in your mind, let go and let God/the Light help you in its manifestation. Give a big sigh of relief as you let go.

* * *

If your seeking opportunity you shall find it. If your seeking friends, you shall find them. If your seeking happiness you shall find it within.

* * *

We need to get to know the true essence of our being—who we really are and who we can be. Seize the golden opportunity that stumbling blocks present to you. Remember that for every problem there is a solution and an opportunity.

* * *

Make a concerted effort to like people and get them to like you. Put a smile in your voice and give them your best smile. Show that you're interested in them and you care about what they're concerned about. It may take some practice but it's worth the effort.

* * *

Learn to develop "people skills". To attain success in life, getting along with people is priority number one. Don't act superior to anyone. Remember the other guy knows more than you do on certain subjects and, can do some things better than you can. That is their individuality. It should be respected and even praised. You can benefit by association with that person. Remember we are all connected by the Light. Give credit where credit is due.

* * *

When the going gets rough—don't quit. Quitters never reach their goals; quitters never succeed. Bad situations block all of us at one time or another. Even the best of us have problems. The difference is: they don't quit. If we quit before we reach our goals, we will fall into the shadows of mediocrity.

* * *

Learn to create circumstances instead of letting circumstances befall you. We can't control all circumstances, but we can control how we respond to them.

* * *

Learn to see the potentialities in everything that crosses your path. Don't put off acting on them. Not to do so could be the greatest mistake of your life. Don't give in to self-doubt. Be an achiever and have confidence in yourself. Seize opportunities when they show themselves and don't let go of them.

* * *

Don't fear failure—it makes us stronger. Where would we be today if it weren't for entrepreneurs who saw a need and filled it, even in the face of adversity.

* * *

When you pursue your goals, remember if one attempt doesn't work –maybe the next one will. All you can do is keep trying until you succeed. For every pitfall there is a solution. Never quit until you've tried all the possibilities.

* * *

Sometimes it is possible that the things we cleave to are holding us back. It could be your job, a bad marriage or your religion. Sooner or later— you'll have to let go or you'll be miserable. Be flexible in your thinking— maybe what you have isn't right for you. Maybe there's something better around the corner.

* * *

Failure teaches us what doesn't work. Concentrate on new possibilities and keep on trying. If you're trying for success—you are a success.

* * *

Don't hesitate to share your ideas with others. They're waiting to help you in your quest. Sometimes you can't succeed by yourself—you need an ally.

* * *

When you're afraid of failure it's not likely that you'll succeed. If you give in to the possibility of failure, you are less equipped for success.

* * *

Potential is the ability to learn and benefit from our mistakes. That makes us leaders in the game of life. Don't give up the fight. You have what it takes to be a leader. See the possibilities that will help you reach your goal.

* * *

Never let anyone discourage you out of your dream. If someone tries to discourage you—simply turn your back on them and go about your business.

* * *

Self-doubt can prevent us from overcoming the barricades that block success. Self-reliance, on the other hand, will help us make the hurdles that lead to success.

* * *

You can't make a half-hearted attempt and expect to succeed. You must give two-hundred per cent in your efforts. Either give all or nothing. Be persistent in everything you do.

* * *

Never give up on your dreams. When you want to quit, just give it one more shot and hope for a miracle. Never take no for an answer. Don't let criticism get you down. Keep your chin up and give it the old college try.

* * *

Create your own future—no one can do it for you. You must do it for yourself.

* * *

To obtain what you desire… find out what the other person wants and help them get it. Then he/she will help you get what you want. You can create your future if you can believe in it.

* * *

We must learn to dominate our thots. Don't let negative thinking dominate you. When we are overwhelmed with doubt and fear, what we fear becomes our reality. Strive to keep all your thots happy and positive and good things will show up in your life.

* * *

Have the fortitude to be the person you want to be. Don't let the judgement of others hold you back.

* * *

Improving your life may be as simple as making a decision. Fold a piece of paper in half. On one side list all the reasons for and on the other side list all the reasons against. This will make it easier to reach a decision.

* * *

What you want from life is waiting for you. Don't allow fear to dissuade you from realizing the things you desire. Fear is but a sick state of mind that can easily be purged and replaced with happy and positive thots.

* * *

Do other people believe in you? That's a pretty good thing. But, there is one very important person that absolutely must believe in you. That person is you. If you don't believe in yourself –how can you expect anyone to follow you?

* * *

If you don't try… you won't succeed. Pull yourself up by your bootstraps and give it a shot. There's no reason not to. Make a list of the things that prevent you from doing what you want to do. Begin working on the smallest and work your way up to the biggest. Do you lack money? That didn't stop Steve Wozniak and Steve Jobs from starting Apple Computers. They scraped together twelve hundred dollars to get their start.

* * *

We all have the potential for success. The difference is that most people don't even try. You must believe in yourself if your going to get anywhere. It is better to try and fail than not to have tried at all. Ignore your fears and try, try, try until you get it right. The only competition worthy of you is yourself. Focus on what's important to you. Persistence is always rewarded.

* * *

Expectation can set us up for disappointment or it can cause manifestation. It depends upon how realistic our goals are and how hard we work at it. How often we visualize having or doing the thing or situation we're asking for is very important. It can help us acquire what we want. The importance of visualization can't be overstressed.

* * *

Be satisfied with what you have, and you will get more. Develop a routine of asking God for what you want and know that the Light will give you what you ask for. In the meantime, take the time to enjoy life and what you have in the present moment.

* * *

Gods law is one abundance. God/the Light wants us to have everything we need. Keep money and material possessions in their proper perspective and know that we are given a surplus to help others. Giving to charity can give us joy. Be grateful that you have been given enough to share. It is more blessed to give than to receive.

* * *

All your daily activities should be like a prayer to glorify God/the Light. It is in our attitude that we make strides to being Godlike.

* * *

Today is a gift—why not embrace it? Do your chores and take time to relax. When we think about the future we can become overwrought. Do the things that today calls for and worry about tomorrow when it comes.

* * *

Let go of the past—turn it over to God/the Light and forget about it. Focus on what you have to do today.

* * *

We are all individuals. Don't try to be like someone else—be the person you're supposed to be. Be the real you. Do the best you can and be satisfied with that. Don't compete with anyone but yourself.

* * *

Make a list of things to do and begin with the most important ones first. Don't be upset if you can't do everything on the list. Just pick up where you left off the next day. Simplify your life and don't try to do more than you can handle. Remember to give yourself time for rest and relaxation.

* * *

Don't be afraid of what might happen—worry can make things happen. God/the light will take care of you and won't let bad things happen to you. All you have to do is trust in the Light and good things will manifest in your life.

* * *

Procrastination can set us up for disappointment, because we didn't do what should have been done. Today is a new day, don't put things off. Today you have been given a fresh start—take advantage of it. If you keep putting things off, you will develop a poor self-image. Set a definite date when you are going to do the things you have been putting off and then—just do it. Do what you can accomplish today and don't put it off till tomorrow.

* * *

Know yourself and be yourself. Don't try to be somebody you don't want to be or don't feel you can be, just to please somebody else. We all have a niche in life where we fit perfectly. If you're comfortable where you are don't force yourself to go any further. There is no substitute for happiness. Don't allow yourself to step out of your comfort zone. But know when there's room for improvement.

* * *

We all need to prioritize and get rid of some of the clutter. Decide what is important and what is less important. Make a list and revise it every week. Choose your battles and ask the Light to guide you in your decisions.

* * *

We should forgive those who have done us wrong. The quicker we do so the better off we are If we balk at-doing so—it adds to the clutter we need to get rid of. If we don't get rid of our anger, we may take it out on someone who doesn't deserve it. Show mercy and compassion to others and don't judge them.

* * *

Learn to be decisive when figuring out problems. Don't hesitate to do what's right. Ask the Light for guidance while meditating, You will know when you get the right answer.

* * *

Think before you speak—those are words of wisdom. How many times have you got into trouble because you just blurted something out without thinking? Think before you speak!

* * *

You can't please everyone all the time—so don't even try. If there's some question about what you should do. Think about what God/the Light would have you do.

* * *

Don't give into fear, it will bring you down and complicate your life. Go into a meditative state and ask for help in confronting your fears. Remember to be grateful for the help.

* * *

There is no sense in arguing with anybody. Where there is disagreement there are no winners. You end up being wrong even when you're right. Be quick to throw in the towel when the conversation starts to get heated.

* * *

Be positive in everything you think say and do. There is no point in being negative. All that does is open the door for more negative ideas and attitudes.

* * *

Be grateful for everything God/the Light has given you. Being thankful helps us to rise to a new plateau where we will get even greater things.

* * *

Pray about everything you do. Ask God/the Light for guidance before making big decisions. Do you really need the thing you're asking for? Or can you do nicely without it? Remember Gods law is one of abundance. But, that does not mean that you should overburden yourself with time payments Save your money until you can pay cash for what you want—if possible.

* * *

We can control our thots and the way we look at things. Many things will not change simply because we want them to. What we must do is take a different approach to the problem or situation. Then just let go and let God/ the Light put the finishing touches on it.

* * *

Never put off till tomorrow what you can do today. If something needs doing—do it now and be done with it. Putting things off until tomorrow, will leave your mind cluttered and will clutter up your day as well.

* * *

Do not complicate your prayers. Keep them plain and simple. Talk to the Light as though you were talking to a person. Remember to give thanks at the end of your prayer.

* * *

Don't be afraid of change—you may encounter some ruts as you effect the transition. But the result makes it all worthwhile. Sometimes you have to give up what you have. But in the final analysis you'll have more than you gave up.

* * *

Instant gratification doesn't always happen—no matter how hard we try. Just be patient and allow God/the Light to do it at the right time. Put your faith in Divine Light and allow things to happen in due time. In the long run, it makes things a lot simpler. Patience and perseverance are worthwhile virtues and should be cultivated. When they are employed difficulties disappear and obstacles vanish.

* * *

Solitude is a win-fall you can give to yourself. If the pressures of daily business leave you feeling frazzled and worn out. Find a quiet place where you can be alone—go into meditation and relax. Take note of any impressions that come to you and act upon them.

* * *

Be generous instead of stingy. The result is you'll be happier. Remember the more you give the more you get.

* * *

How we approach life and view the circumstances surrounding it is our choice. Choose to be happy and positive, rather than negative and gloomy. Life is too short to sit around brooding. Life is what you make it—so be happy and enjoy life.

* * *

Our thots have the power to create whatever we're thinking about. So be careful about your thinking—for you are forecasting your future. Think positive, happy thots and watch them blossom into reality.

* * *

Take your life to new heights, by adjusting your thinking to something positive. Negative thots will bring you down into the abyss. Remember when one door of opportunity closes God/the Light will open another.

* * *

If you perceive a problem in your life don't accentuate it by dwelling on it. Think in reverse and say: "I am happy, I am healthy, I am strong, I can do things I couldn't do yesterday, today is going to be a great day and good things are coming to me.". As you develop this attitude on the inside—God/ the Light will make it manifest on the outside.

* * *

God/the Light will never fail you or let you down. The Light will always be there for you. Don't be fearful the Light won't let bad things happen to you—if you keep that first and foremost in your mind.

* * *

Shirk off your disappointments like you would an old coat. Keep on trying and if it doesn't work… try again. Say to yourself: "My time has arrived and I'm going to start today.". Be passionate about what you're doing. Every set back and disappointment puts you closer to attaining your goals. Be grateful for what God/the Light has done for you so far; and for the inspiration to do better.

* * *

Each day we are given a gift… don't squander it! Life is like a puzzle, you might not see the picture until you fit certain pieces together. So it is with your life—you may not see what you're waiting for until you've reached a certain stage in your journey. Wait and see what your higher- self and the Light have in store for you.

* * *

Program your mind to be exceptional. Every day put two-hundred per cent into the task at hand. Do everything as though you're blessed—and you will be! Back all your aspirations with action.

* * *

No difficulties are impossible to surmount. Just turn the problem over to the Light and watch what happens! Your problem will dissipate into thin air.

* * *

Belief and knowing are the same thing. It is essential that you "know" when doing your thot forms. At this point, you can become complacent—knowing that your prayers will be answered, in due time. Yes, your thot forms are prayers and God answers every legitimate prayer What does legitimate mean? In this case, it means something that will benefit others besides yourself and do no harm to anybody.

* * *

Maybe it's time to encourage someone... do you know somebody who is struggling to get by? Or maybe you know someone who is starting a business venture. Tell them that you think they're great and they can do anything they set their mind to. Give them all the encouragement you can.

* * *

Choose faith over fear—fear begets more problems—while faith fosters opportunity. Meditate and pray for happiness to come into your life. Think of the blessings you've already received and the blessings that are coming to you. Be grateful for what you have.

* * *

Procrastination is a bad habit that can get out of control. If you put off one thing—pretty soon you're putting off a lot of things. And, your life can become utter chaos. Why not take a day off and tomorrow you'll find you're full of energy, and will be able to catch up on all the things you have to do. Make a list and start with the smaller jobs and work your way up.

* * *

Do you think of God/the Light when you wake up? It's a good idea to remember the Light thru-out the day. It will make your tasks easier and put a song in your heart. Just take a few minutes to remember you are not alone.

* * *

Focus on what you want—not on what you don't want. Your thinking has a tremendous impact on your reality. Visualize good things happening to you. Counter all negative thots by dismissing them and substituting positive affirmations.

* * *

Take what you have and do the best you can with it. Don't let obstacles get you down. Simply find a way to go around them. Nothing is going to change until you change it. So, keep your chin up and go in fighting.

* * *

Be happy with the little things life has to offer. Accept what you've been given and learn to enjoy it. Remember to be appreciative for what you have and give thanks for it. Enjoying the life, you've been given is a matter of choice. So, make a decision to make the most of what you've been given.

* * *

It's a good idea to pray your way thru the day. Say things like: "Thank you for this glorious day. Thank you for your strength and guidance. Thank you for taking care of my children. Or, please help do this job quickly and efficiently". Just simple little prayers like these will remind you that God/ the Light is always with you- ready and willing to help you with every little thing.

* * *

We all have the option to like or not like whatever we are doing. All it takes is change our focus. You can make the decision to be happy or frustrated. It's up to you whether or not you enjoy the thing you're doing. You need to prep yourself before doing anything. Go into a brief meditative state and see yourself doing what needs to be done and doing it well. Then thank the Light for helping you.

* * *

Laughter is the best medicine—it reduces anxiety and depression. It releases chemicals into our system that relieve pain and give us a sense of well-being.

* * *

Be excited for everything you have. Once it has passed—you can never recover it. Say: "Today is going to be a great day and I am ready for good things to happen!"

* * *

Everybody needs somebody to lean on. Maybe it's your spouse or lover, a family member, your best friend or a minister. But you need somebody to tell your dreams and aspirations to. Or maybe you just need to get something off your chest. How about talking to God/the Light? The Light is always there for you and is available twenty-four hours a day. Knowing this—you should never be lonely.

* * *

Enthusiasm, perseverance and visualization are the cornerstones of success.

* * *

Maybe things aren't going your way or situations aren't turning out the way you'd hoped. Is it worth giving up your peace of mind for? You may not be able to control circumstances, but you can control the way you react to them. Remain positive and happy about what is going on in your life. Work your way around obstacles and pray for help in resolving your problems.

* * *

When some aggravated person tries to dump on you simply say: "God bless you." and walk away.

* * *

Put a smile on your face and you will cutdown on anxiety and depression and you'll be happier.

* * *

What you show to others will come back to you. If you give everyone a smile, you'll get smiles in return. Smiles will enhance your demeanor. It's hardly possible to be in a bad mood and smile at the same time. Smiling is contagious.

* * *

Say to yourself: "I am meant to go higher and higher. I accept the fact that I am supposed to be where I am right now, but I am moving up. I may be moving at snail's pace but I will get where I'm going—sooner or later. In the mean-time I'll be the best I can be right where I am."

* * *

Life is not about attaining goals so much as how we conduct ourselves on the way to attaining those goals. When you have accomplished them, there will be other goals. If you are ill conceived in your thots and believe your goal is everything and all else is subordinate to the goal. You are mistaken and are missing the best things life has to offer. Enjoy each day as it comes. Don't waste your life straining to reach a goal and missing what life has to offer.

Find your happiness in the little things life has to offer and you'll be happier by far. Accomplishing your goals will give you an immense sense of purpose. But, that's not all there is to life. It's not the getting but the getting there that's important. Slow down and enjoy life as it happens.

* * *

Make your friends and family number one in your life. Give them top priority. You never know when one of them might be taken from you. Let them know you appreciate them and thank them for the help they give you. When you come to the end of your life, your job and your career won't be sitting there holding your hand—but your friends and family will.

* * *

Slow down and enjoy the trip. Don' put all your energy into your work. Save some of it for your family and friends. Enjoy the journey and all life has to offer. You'll still arrive at the same destination and you'll be happier because you took the time to smell the roses.

* * *

Learn to appreciate the things you've been given: a healthy body, good vision, your spouse, your children, your car, your house… the list can go on and on. The point is you have a lot to be thankful for.

* * *

Have you made mistakes you still feel guilty about? God/the Light has already forgiven you. Now it's time to forgive yourself. It's in the past and you've learned your lesson. It's time to get over it. You've made some bad decisions but, you made more right decisions. Stop punishing yourself and focus on doing what's right from now on.

* * *

Don't allow people in your life who try to limit you for their own purpose—whatever that might be. It is easy to become dependent on someone to take up your slack. It is much better to stand on your own two feet. Once you get your feet wet, it's time to do things on your own. God /the Light has given you all that you require to do the task at hand. You don't need someone to tell you what to do and when to do it. You'll raise your self-esteem when you do things on your own.

* * *

Do you worry about what other people think of you? Do you seek to please them just to get their approval? Of course, we all want to make a good impression on others. But don't go overboard. Don't come up to others expectations. Come up to your own standards. Don' let anybody mold you into someone you're not.

Be the best person you can be. Don't try to emulate others and wind up being phony. Just be happy being yourself. Learn to like yourself and others will gravitate towards you. Be thrilled to be just the way you are.

* * *

Someone may have hurt you deeply in the past; and you still haven't gotten over it. The bad memory is festering inside you. Now it's time to let go of the memory. You must forgive the person that harmed you. Rest assured that persons bad Karma will catch up with him/her sooner or later. What you have to do is forget and release the bad memory. Conjure a good memory to replace it. Bad memories can literally make you sick—if you don't get rid of them. So, let go and let God.

* * *

Don't be a gossip. What another person does is none of your business. How would you like it if someone gossiped about you? Being critical can stop you from attaining your goals. Judge not lest you be judged. Never judge another person until you've walked a mile in their shoes.

* * *

Help others to succeed in their endeavors. By doing so, you're better equipped to attain success in your own efforts. Everybody needs encouragement.

* * *

The world around us is not governed by our perceptions; but by our interpretation of those perceptions. In other words: our reality is not based on what we see but, by what we conceive it to be.

* * *

The secret of happiness is to choose to be happy. We are what we think. We can choose to be happy or we can choose to be sad. The choice is up to us.

* * *

A strong sense of direction will enable us to reach our goals almost without any effort.

* * *

Our intent determines the path we shall follow. If our purpose is to just get by then we will end up where we started. On the other hand, when we have our goals firmly implanted in our minds and are determined to overcome all obstacles –we will eventually reach our destination. Providing we are persistent in our efforts.

* * *

It is beneficial to believe in something. But, keep it to yourself unless asked for it. It is never a good idea to push your beliefs off on others. Respect their right to think and choose on their own.

* * *

Accomplishment is not determined by a single act, but by a series of small steps.

* * *

People are characteristically drawn to people who are happy and smile a lot.

* * *

Goals and objectives will take us from where we are to where we want to be. Places we didn't think were even possible.

* * *

Change is inevitable—all we can do is change with circumstances that occur in our life; so we can take advantage of them and make them work for us. Look for the possibilities that lie hidden in those circumstances. When something appears to be out of balance look to see if it adds to the stability of the whole. If you have faith in the results of your endeavors— what you believe will come to pass. The seeds you sow will grow to bear fruit. We may have to change before we can change outside circumstances. Our ultimate power is the ability to decide how people and circumstances will affect us.

* * *

If we see things from an objective point of view, we can subconsciously impose our intentions on other people. Which is not necessarily a bad thing. When we think that something is a problem, that thot is the problem for there is only opportunity in perceived problems.

* * *

In your quest for leadership you will encounter things that test your ability. Praise and rewards will come to you—as you effectively deal with these challenges.

* * *

If you wait for things to happen—they will happen. Take the bull by the horns and get it over with. Seek out your enemies and listen to their point of view with empathy. That alone can resolve the problem.

* * *

Your discipline comes from within. You are motivated by the source of your being (your higher self). To do what's right, listen to that voice and let it guide you.

* * *

By using our imagination, we can visualize ourselves attaining the potentialities that abide within us and see them to fruition. This possibility exists thru Divine law and cannot be refuted.

* * *

We live too much in the past and not enough in our imaginations.

* * *

Your decisions concerning circumstance makes you who you are. Your moral values must be in harmony with the principles of the society we live in. Therefore, we will make the right decisions and will attain peace within.

* * *

Set a good example by defining success according to your standards. Create your future by using visualization. Show respect for the other guy and respect yourself. Forgive yourself for past mistakes.

* * *

Stop complaining about the way things are and do something to change them. Stop sitting around thinking about the obstacles and do something about it. Get up and do it!

* * *

Don't worry about what others are thinking about you—instead worry about what you think about yourself. You must have a good self-image or you'll get nowhere. Learn to be your own best friend. Look in the mirror and say: "I think you're a great person and I believe in you! You can do anything you set your mind to.".

Whatever you focus on will be attracted to you. That's the simple Law of Attraction. Science has proven that everything in the universe is vibrating at one frequency or another. Those vibrations can cause a manifestation in your life—for good or bad. So, it's obvious that we must discipline our thinking—for our thots are also vibrations that can attract like vibrations.

* * *

The more you concentrate on what you do want—the faster it will become manifest In your life. Write your goals down and set a realistic deadline for accomplishing them. Go thru your list as many times a day as is possible. Try to visualize them and experience the emotions you will feel when you've accomplished your goal. If you have your privacy vocalize your intention.

* * *

Once you have visualized what you want—picture the steps you'll need to take to accomplish your goal. Then take action. Without action your goals are just daydreams.

* * *

Granted, sometimes what you visualize will just fall into your lap. But, for the most part –you must work for it. Very seldom do you get something for nothing. However, your visualizations will make things easier for you.

* * *

Failure in your endeavor is to be expected, when just starting out. Failure contains a lesson—what not to do the next time you try. Keep striving towards your goal. Every failure gives you information you can use in your next attempt.

* * *

You have to confront your fears, or you'll never get anywhere. Make a list of things you're afraid of and confront the least of them and work your way up to the biggest one. Procrastination makes things appear worse than they actually are. Don't put off until tomorrow what you can do today.

* * *

Persistence is the key to success in almost everything. So, don't give up—keep on trying—no matter how many times you fail. Pick yourself up and get back in the race.

* * *

Allocate time at the end of the day to focus on the events that transpired during the day. Go over your wins and losses. Make note of the lessons you've learned and make plans for the coming day. This is a good time to do your thot-forms and positive affirmations.

* * *

Save ten per cent of your income. This will give you emergency funds if you need them. It will also allow you to pay cash for things you would otherwise have to finance. Or maybe you could use the money to start your own business.

* * *

Enthusiasm lets you see the focal points you will need to succeed. It comes from within and cannot be quenched. When you are filled with enthusiasm your imagination is stimulated and your efforts will be influenced by your inner self. You will take a passionate approach to the task at hand. Success comes from enjoying what you do. No worthwhile goal can be achieved without enthusiasm. Make a firm commitment to accomplish your goal and take the first step on your journey to happiness and fulfillment.

* * *

When you are doing what you love—you're already a success!

* * *

Include other people in your life. Find a friend who has the same interests you do. Exchange information and ideas. It would be nice if you could create a circle of friends who could give you input concerning your pet project. Maybe you could all meet twice a month—that would be good for you and good for them as well.

* * *

If you're just starting out on a venture, you could use a mentor. Choose somebody who is already successful in your chosen field. Give them a call and tell them you're interested in knowing what it was like when they were first starting out. Ask if you can ask them a few questions. People like talking about themselves. Ask it you can call back and ask a few more questions. This way you can initiate a relationship and maybe even get a few contact referrals.

* * *

Always remember to tell the truth—no matter how hard it's going to be. It's much easier than getting caught in a lie.

* * *

Let other people know you appreciate them. It may be a phone call, a thank you note, a small gift, lunch or brunch or simply paying attention when they talk.

* * *

Be faithful in keeping your promises to yourself and others. If you don't, you'll have low self-esteem and more self-doubt. Put your promises in writing, the minute you make them, so you don't forget. Also make a habit to be early for appointments.

* * *

When doing your thot forms try to incorporate the feelings and emotion you will feel when you have the thing or situation you so desire. Try to summon the sensations of touching, feeling or smelling etc.

* * *

You must get rid of your limiting beliefs—because they are holding you back. It doesn't matter where they came from (parents, friends, or spouse). The fact is they are holding you back—forcing you to have a life of mediocrity. Make a list of things or situations you would like to have if you could have anything and everything you wanted. Read thru it three times a day.

* * *

Find a need and fill it. Do you have a pet peeve? Can you do anything about it? Can you make money from it? How much time and money would it cost you to do something about it?

Ari

* * *

Don't take no for an answer. If you run into a roadblock—take a detour.

* * *

Anything the mind can conceive, you can achieve.

* * *

Every adversity contains the potential for greater benefit.

* * *

You can create anything you can imagine.

* * *

Ever atom in the entire universe began as a form of energy resonating at different frequencies. Your goals and desires are thot impulses which are forms of energy. Ideas are products of your imagination; as such they can be directed to your subconscious mind for fruition.

* * *

Persistence is the key to success in everything you do. Winners never quit—quitters never win.

* * *

An equal advantage comes with every failure. Turn defeat into victory. Persistence means not taking no for an answer. Don't let discouragement get you down. Never quit pursuing your goals.

* * *

There are restraints that will prevent you from attaining your objectives. You must establish a plan of action that will take you thru the resistances;

so that when they appear, you can overcome them. Accept problems as challenges and you will beat them and come out being a winner.

* * *

The more you visualize your goal the easier it will be to devise a strategy to attain that goal. List the steps you will have to take to reach your destiny. Some-times the future looks bleak until you focus on taking the first step and then the next step and then another...

* * *

By using positive affirmations, you are programming your subconscious mind to achieve success. Also, you are crowding out the negative thots that have been holding you back.

* * *

The subconscious mind works best when the conscious mind is happily occupied either at play or at rest. If you don't refresh your mind, it is not possible to feel rejuvenated. A sufficient amount of time at play is critical for the mind to be productive.

* * *

To reach a higher plane, we must adopt new habits and get rid of the old bad habits. It won't take long for the new habits to replace the old ones.

* * *

You are as you think you are. You may have personality defects that originated during childhood or they have come from the experience of a bad marriage or perhaps you may have been take advantage of at your place of employment. Regardless of where they came from they must be eliminated. Use positive affirmations to get rid of the old flaws in your personality. You are the way you are because of the way you see yourself—it has a hold on you –because your subconscious has accepted these old ideas as being true. From now on see yourself as you want to be. When the old flaws appear, dismiss them telling them they no longer have power over you. Say positive affirmations to replace the negative thot. Affirmations when repeated take form in your subconscious and are accepted as true and will change your personality for the better.

* * *

Your way of doing things is the direct result of your thinking.

* * *

The best thing you can do for others is to make the most of your own life.

* * *

We are all the product of our thots. Believe in yourself—see yourself doing things in a big way and you will do things in a big way. Make your mind work for you instead of against you. Think in terms of success and start doing it right now. Think of yourself as a success in the now as well as in future. Believe in yourself and think your way into prosperity. Think in terms of success and not in terms of failure or mediocrity. Think in terms of achievement and accomplishment.

* * *

The degree of accomplishment you will achieve is in direct correlation to what you believe is possible. When faced with an opportunity always think in terms of "I can" never think in terms of "I can't". Thinking in terms of "I can do it" conditions your mind to think of yourself as an achiever and a success.

Fear can stop you from accomplishing your goals. It is the primary enemy of success. It will turn you away from opportunity and can even make you sick. It can make you nervous and tongue tied. It can cause you to turn down opportunities. Fear can also cause depression and anxiety and can stop you DEAD in your tracks. Indecision and procrastination can feed your fear. What can we do about it?

Action can dispel your fear. Face up to your dilemma. Create a plan of action and implement it right away. Don't hesitate to make changes to your plans.

Separate your fear from other thots. What exactly are you afraid of? What can you do about it? There is a solution to every problem. Procrastination only makes your problem look bigger than it is.

Program your subconscious mind to remember all the good positive things you did in a similar situation. This will bolster your confidence and dissuade negative thots.

* * *

What do you do with negative thots? Banish them! Tell them they have no place in your life and are welcome to leave and not come back. Substitute a positive affirmation.

* * *

Is temerity a problem for you? From now on pay attention to your posture—keep your shoulders back and your spine straight and stretch yourself to your full height. When you walk pick up the pace a little. Give others a firm handshake and look them in the eye and give them a smile. By acting as tho you have confidence, you will instill the feeling of confidence within you. In meetings don't be afraid to express your opinion and ask questions. Practice these simple steps every day and soon you will become the confident person you've always wanted to be.

* * *

People like to feel important. It costs nothing to call them by name and give them a compliment. Finally, give them a genuine smile. Always give people more than they anticipate getting.

* * *

The only way to get things started is in acting. Think about the steps you must take to do the task before you; and then just do it! Taking action instils confidence and dispels fear. Don't put off until tomorrow what you can do today. Thinking in terms of doing something later can constitute failure.

* * *

Waiting for perfect conditions is a form of procrastination. Expect hardships and obstacles along the way. Simply find a way around them. Doing so will make you stronger and add to your confidence.

* * *

Problems can't be solved if you think they're unsolvable. Think about solutions and try again. Keep trying until you get it right. Sometimes we get to close to the problem and we can't see the solution. Back off for a while and when you get back to the problem approach it from a new perspective.

* * *

Everything on this earth and inner space was visualized before it became a reality. Every accomplishment is achieved by a series of small tasks achieved one step at a time. The step by step process is the only smart way to attain any goal.

* * *

See to it that you have time to yourself to think problems and situations over. Our mind shapes our opinions which shape our reality. Close your self off in a quiet place and meditate to get solutions to your problems.

* * *

When you mix persistence with a burning desire for a thing or situation, you can achieve anything you so desire. By applying known techniques thots can be converted into riches.

* * *

One of the first principles of success is knowing what you want. The thots which we have that dominate our thinking will attract the right people and situations to us. But, you must be prepared for it and have something to offer (goods or service). Nobody gets something for nothing. Dreams do not manifest when our lives are dominated by procrastination or laziness.

* * *

When belief is homogenized with action, there is nothing we cannot achieve. The subconscious mind picks up the thot and conveys it to Cosmic Intelligence. We might call this process of thinking: prayer. This method of affirmation cannot be defeated by hard luck or obstacles, because we can simply go around the blocks in our path.

* * *

Any thot which is repeated is accepted by the subconscious mind as fact and will bring about its physical counterpart—by the most practical means available. Believing is the basis for all manifestations. This goes beyond all scientific explanation. Believing puts one in direct communion with Universal Mind. The subconscious mind can attract things that have similar resonance.

* * *

We are the product of our thinking. Thoughts spiced with emotion beget corresponding thots. The process of manifesting our desires works because we have the power to program our subconscious mind. Thus, bringing the conditions favorable to the completion of our goals.

* * *

Don't be influenced by the opinions of others. If you are, you may not be successful in your chosen undertaking. You have a mind of your own; you have reached your conclusions thru careful and deliberate thinking. Don't let others dissuade you from accomplishing the task at hand. It's good idea to keep your plans to yourself—except for your mentor and those who give you good sound advice and ideas. Remember that your actions speak louder than words. In short—keep your mouth shut and go about your business—smug in the fact that you will succeed.

* * *

Persistence is the key to everything you want to accomplish. Sure, there will be stumbling blocks along the way, to be certain. But, that shouldn't be a problem for you. You'll just find a way around them. There is a seed of opportunity hidden within every problem. Every cloud has a silver lining. Just keep on trying and trying and try again.

* * *

Persistence, concentrated effort and a definite sense of purpose are the three ingredients that will guaranty success in any endeavor.

* * *

You can channel your sexual energy into creative energy if you so desire. It's just a matter of will power. This will enable you to come up with solutions to your problems; and will take you to a higher level in your chosen vocation or avocation. Particularly in your artistic endeavors.

* * *

Information received from the creative mind is more reliable than information contained in the conscious mind—because it is limited by experience, and not all knowledge garnered from experience is reliable. However, the creative mind is linked to Universal Mind thru the creative currents.

* * *

The human mind may be stimulated by channeling sexual energies into the task at hand. When channeled thru the creative mind this energy will take you to a higher plane on which you can solve problems in a scientific manner or by speculating and postulating.

* * *

Enthusiasm for what you're doing will speed you towards success. Coupled with gratitude you have an unbeatable team.

* * *

Worry is a terrible thing it can incapacitate you and leave you depressed and full of fear and anxiety. Come to terms with the fact that life can be conquered, and you can make things go your way. Repeat positive affirmations and go into a state of meditation to find the solution to your problems. Visualize the steps you will take to resolve the problems and then take action.

* * *

You can control your mind—don't let negative ideas control you. Exercise self-discipline and banish negative thots. Stay busy with a clearly defined purpose. Come up with a concrete plan for attaining your goals. Direct yourself to achieve specific objectives by laying out the stepping stones that carry you to the realization of your objective.

* * *

Do you think you don't have time to devote to your project? Ask yourself this question: "How can I do more?". Creative answers will come to you. There are many things you can delegate to others, leaving you with more time to do the important things. Organize your schedule so you can do similar things at a specific time—like returning phone calls, dictating letters etcetera.

* * *

Ideas only have value when they're acted upon. Be a doer—not a talker.

* * *

Fix firmly in your mind where you want to be a year from now; five years from now. Write out an accomplishment plan (what you need to do to accomplish your goal). Make a decision to achieve your goal. Remember you can only take one step at a time. Each small task will take you closer to achieving what you want. Take a different plan of action as circumstances dictate.

* * *

Achieving thru the act of creation is a good beginning towards accomplishing your goals. Begin with the attitude "I can" and surmount it with the statement "I will". At this point you have made a commitment to yourself to accomplish the seemingly impossible. Remember you are only limited by the laws of time and nature. You are never too old or too young. You are not limited by gender or nationality. All that is necessary is that you focus on your goal and take the first step to attaining your hearts desire.

* * *

Be prepared—as your go on your journey to your objective—to meet obstacles on the way to your goal. Anticipate them before hand and come up with solutions; so, you can just wipe them aside as though they were nothing. In doing so you will develop a high degree of self-confidence; that will spur on to even greater heights.

* * *

Enthusiasm is a powerful force. It will make your work easier. It can add substance to your thot forms. It can get you promoted and can win you friends. How do you get enthusiasm? By being happy and having an incentive that will bring you happiness. It is easy to be happy… all you have to do is meditate on your goals and accomplishments.

* * *

You must have an objective in life and it must be specific. Develop a plan of action to achieve your goal. Imagine the obstacles that would stand in your way and take the time to see your way over or around them. Now you're on your way to success. Stair step smaller objectives to achieve your goal. Accept all problems as challenges and remember every obstacle has the seed of opportunity hidden within it.

* * *

Break all your goals—large or small—into fundamental parts. Sit back and see the whole picture. Then focus on the thing you must do first—breaking it down to its components—then have at it. When you're done go to the next step and do it the same way.

* * *

How do we form new habits? By eliminating its negative counterpart and substituting positive affirmations to take the place of the undesirable negative habit. Then consciously do the thing you want to do. Do it with authority and tell yourself "There I've done it and I'm going to do it this way from now on.". Keep repeating this pattern until you start doing it subconsciously.

* * *

Procrastination will rob you of the future you so richly deserve. See yourself as someone who does things in the now—not the future. Back your intentions with action. Attack the task at hand with enthusiasm and be persistent in acting on your plans for the future.

* * *

Sometimes we invest our energies to evade bad results rather than remarkable outcomes. Change your focus from what you don't want to what you do want. You can give yourself a push in the right direction, stand still or go backwards, the choice is up to you.

* * *

Others see you the way you see yourself. Others will treat you the way you treat yourself. It's up to you to show others they need to respect you and treat you with courtesy.

* * *

You have the option to choose the degree of excellence you will experience in your life. You can attain a higher level of existence if you believe you can.

* * *

Whatever concept you have in respect to God—you must open yourself up to it and invite it to become a part of your life. You can do this thru meditation. Feel the presence of that higher power in your heart and experience it thru the emotion of gratitude. You can find no greater ally than God/the Light in the presence of God/the Light you will feel exalted.

* * *

What others may think of you is only their opinion and has nothing to do with your self-worth.

* * *

First you must set your goals, then establish the highlights that will take you towards completion. Set the stepping stones that will take you to the highlights. Change your plans as circumstances dictate. Make sure that your goal will benefit others besides yourself and will do no harm to anyone. Move forward with the full knowledge that Cosmic intelligence is helping you along the way.

* * *

As you are on the way to accomplishing your goal. Seek out others who are doing the same thing. Ask them to act as your mentors and give you advise as you strive towards your goal. Find out what mistakes they made and what they did right. Their advice can save you hundreds of hours and thousands of dollars and a heap of frustration.

* * *

Determination is very important it will help you thru the rough spots and will help you grow in character as well. Take it nice and easy with the determination that you will reach your goals.

* * *

Keep a scrapbook of things you want and want to do. Use catalogs, brochures and magazines—cut the pictures out and glue them to the pages. Go thru the scrapbook at least once a day.

* * *

To achieve determination, you must focus on the task at hand and shut out all distractions Don't let bad circumstances drag you under. Just concentrate on what you're doing It's not the circumstances that matter, it's how you react to them that counts.

* * *

When you are connected to a higher purpose, you begin to attract opportunities and individuals who can help you along the way. You begin to acquire the qualities you want for yourself and repel the traits you don't want to keep.

* * *

Instead of focusing on your problems. Fix your gaze on remedies for the situation.

* * *

You must be cognizant of where you are and where you want to be. Create a strategy to obtain your goal and then go for it!

* * *

You can't accomplish anything in life if you don't take action. Having a desire is not enough. It is just the first step in attaining your goal. The second step is planning the steps you will take. The next step is preparing yourself and doing the necessary things to get yourself ready for accomplishing your goal. The final step is to take action, going around the obstacles that get in your way.

* * *

Commitment to your goals is essential in any undertaking. Without commitment you'll flounder and fail when you meet your first obstacle. That's where persistence comes in. No matter how many times you hear "no" keep fighting. Sooner or later you'll attain your goal. Combine enthusiasm with persistence and there's no way you can't win.

* * *

Happiness and success are not manifest by accident nor are they a matter of luck. They must be worked for and strived for. They are a matter of choice. You must choose to attain them, and you must labor to get them, and must extend yourself to obtain them.

* * *

When you are not honest with others, they will eventually find you out. And you've potentially lost a friend. When you lie constantly, you won't remember what's true and what isn't.

* * *

Set your goals and bring your future into the now of your existence. That is where you can take action to create the future you desire.

* * *

People who don't set goals are just wandering around aimlessly. You must have an objective if you are to reach your full potential.

* * *

In achieving your goals, some of the more important things you can do are planning and preparation and having the right attitude. You must have a clearly defined objective and a deadline for its manifestation. You have the potential to accomplish more than you think you can. Just remember the sky's the limit. You must react to the opportunities that present themselves; and you must act in an expeditious manner. Remember the early bird gets the worm.

* * *

One reason so many people fail to reach their goals is they're afraid to take the risk. They would rather bathe in the light of mediocrity. That is not to put them down for not wanting to get ahead. As a matter of fact—in one sense, it is to be admired when someone is happy with what they have. You—on the other hand—wouldn't be reading this book, if you didn't want to get more out of life.

* * *

Past mistakes are of value because we can learn from them and can avoid repeating them. When we make the wrong decisions, we surround ourselves, with circumstances that could otherwise be avoided. When that happens, we must look for the seeds of potential that we can take advantage of.

* * *

Do you hesitate to strive for goals because you're afraid you might not reach them? If you take small steps one at a time and are persistent in your efforts, you will reach your goals.

* * *

It may seem safer not to put your goals in writing –because if you fail there no written evidence that you had a goal and didn't reach it –but that's just hog wash! All your doing is fooling yourself. If you don't set your goals in writing you're setting yourself up for failure. By putting something down on paper—you're making a commitment to yourself.

* * *

It's better to take a risk and fail, than not to have tried at all. If you fail—you've learned what not to do, the next time you try. Remember persistence puts you on the road to success.

* * *

Don't let the opinions of others restrain or restrict your intentions to attain you goal. Some people would like confine you to mediocrity. Because misery loves company.

* * *

Falling down as you strive to achieve your goals is to be expected. What's important is that you get backup after you fall. How's your motivation? Are you prepared to be persistent as you make an effort achieve your goals? Do you have the inner drive—it takes to attain your goals?

* * *

Be sure to meditate every day and ask for guidance along the way.

* * *

Be excited and remain positive about what you're doing. There will be circumstances that can set you back. But you can stay on track and continue on your journey towards your destination.

* * *

You are who are and where you are because of your thinking.

* * *

Our beliefs control our thinking and produce emotions that affect our decisions. Our decisions have a strong effect on our lives in general.

* * *

If you want to be a winner in the game of life, you must think like a winner. You are as you think you are.

* * *

Taking care of your physical body is essential to your wellbeing. Proper diet and exercise should be part of your daily routine.

* * *

We all have the potential for failure or for greatness. It's up to us what we achieve. The keys to greatness are persistence, enthusiasm and visualization.

* * *

A wholesome self-image is the focal point for success and happiness. Self-image is the essence of your potential for achievement and contentment. Self-image is very important when dealing with people because they can pick up on the attitude you have towards yourself and will treat you accordingly.

* * *

Dedication s more important than education.

* * *

We have an obligation and responsibility to do the right thing—even when no one is watching.

* * *

You must have a clearly defined set of goals or you'll never get anywhere. Put them on paper and set a deadline for their accomplishment. Goals equip you to accomplish more.

* * *

Obstacles can become stepping stones. As you go on your journey towards your goal, you may have to compensate or make adjustments due to circumstances. But you will still reach your goal, providing you are persistent in your efforts.

* * *

Dedication, determination and discipline are necessary if you are to reach your goals.

Printed in the United States
By Bookmasters